Mental Toughness Training for Volleyball:
Maximizing Technical and Mental Mechanics

Mike Voight, Ph.D.
Sport Psychology-Performance Consultant

ISBN: 1-58518-942-1
Library of Congress Control Number: 2005929562
Cover design: Jeanne Hamilton
Book layout: Jeanne Hamilton
Front cover photo: Courtesy of USC Sports Information

Coaches Choice
P.O. Box 1828
Monterey, CA 93942
www.coacheschoice.com

Dedication

As always, to my H & S, Jenny, BC, and our twins, Allyson Eileen and
Julieann Morgan

To all the coaches and players who have educated me about the
great game of volleyball, especially those from the Trojan volleyball family

Acknowledgments

I am indebted to those who have assisted me with this 2nd book: Jim Peterson, Kristi Huelsing, and staff at Coaches Choice; my bro who is always an unbelievable source of support; USC Sports Information, especially Tim Tessalone; the coaches who gave of their time to read the book and offer important feedback; all the volleyballers who have shared their games and life stories with me through the years; all the head coaches that I have been so privileged to work with, including Lisa Love, Mick Haley, Jerritt Elliott, Nancy Somera, Paula Weishoff, Erikka Gulbranson, Ann Leonard-House, Liz Towne-Gilbert, and Chris Keif.

Contents

Foreword

A great coach once said, "the joy of coaching a team with great chemistry is matched only by the frustration of coaching a team with poor chemistry." Through the years, I have attended hundreds of clinics that spent hours on how to pass a ball, setting techniques, and hitting efficiency. Seldom did I find information on "training mental toughness" or "maximizing technical and mental mechanics." And yet, when it comes to being successful, these are the things that coaches refer to most in describing their teams' victories or defeats.

In volleyball, skills are extremely important to success. Because the sport is a "rebound" sport, many hours of repetition must be spent perfecting the techniques needed to control the ball. But when the game starts, it is the mental toughness and the "feel good" quality that allow athletes to play fearless and give their best effort for the team. To develop toughness and this "feel good" united front, many hours need to be spent working on these particular components to get everyone on the same page.

Much of the information that is presented in this book has been used with great success here at USC. Mike Voight presents a very organized and easy-to-apply template of team building and mental toughness training. As we have shown on the court, it works! This training is beneficial for the collective team and for each individual player when applied on a consistent basis with good planning. Mental strength is something you can feel when watching a contest, and Mike has captured its components perfectly.

I know the applications and techniques in this book will be a great help to your team too. Best of luck!

Courtesy of USC Sports Information

Mick Haley
Head Women's Volleyball Coach
University of Southern California
National Champions 2002 & 2003
AVCA Coach of the Year 2003

Introduction

The primary purpose of this book is to bring to light the importance of the mental aspects of playing and excelling in volleyball. So much has been published on improving the physical side of a volleyball player's development (strength and conditioning), as well as the technical and strategic (skills and strategy) aspects. There is good reason for this, as these are the basics every player must have as part of his game. But an often-ignored area not addressed in coaching books, videos, and seminars is the mental part of a player's game. In fact, there are very few resources that volleyball coaches can turn to that specifically address mental training for their players. The following scenarios should give you a better idea what is meant by the mental side of volleyball. The number in parentheses indicates where this area is addressed in the book.

- Players who think too much instead of just playing (Chapter 2)
- Players who are great performers at practice yet cannot apply what they've learned come game time (Chapter 3).
- Teams or players that are consistently "slow starters" (Chapter 4).
- Players or teams that are inconsistent due to poor fitness or technical problems (Chapter 5).
- Players who are not truly committed to the team goals and standards (Chapter 6).
- Players who try to aim and force their shots, thus changing their technical mechanics (Chapter 7).
- Players who do not adequately fuel or hydrate themselves (Chapter 8).
- Players who seem to "forget" plays when they knew them all week in practice (Chapter 9).
- Teams who cannot seem to get "on the same page" (Chapter 10).
- A coach who tells a reporter that his players were just "not ready" for this game (Chapter 11).
- An outside hitter who consistently gets very anxious prior to big games, and thus performs poorly (Chapter 12).
- Teams that go through the motions in the majority of practices (Chapter 13).
- Coaches who are unsure that mental training can be utilized with club players (Chapter 14).

This book attempts to go beyond the conditioning, and beyond the X's and O's, by revealing an overlooked part of playing sound volleyball—the mental game. This book introduces numerous concepts, including mental mechanics, performance barriers, expanding player capacities, mechanical breakdowns, automaticity of performance, and mental-skills training strategies. The information contained within is derived from the author's experience consulting with top performers in the sport, as well as from the most current research and applications from the sport science fields, including sport psychology, motor development, pedagogy, strength and conditioning, and exercise physiology.

This book is organized for those coaches who have specific issues in mind, and also for those who want a broader view of all that the mental game entails. Some coaches may be dealing with some team issues and want to access this information immediately, whether it is the barriers that could be limiting team potential or actual team-intervention strategies that can be implemented right away. The book evolves from the theoretical to the practical, with Section 1 detailing what toughness is, Section 2 explaining the barriers to optimal performance, and Section 3 presenting proven training techniques used by top coaches, athletes, and sport psychology consultants to combat these barriers. Numerous figures, survey instruments, and feedback forms are included to better equip coaches with the necessary tools to combat performance barriers of all kinds. Finally, since there are so many inspirational sport heroes representing different levels and sports, specific examples and quotes from these sources are shared throughout the book. Competitive athletes and coaches should find inspiration on a daily basis, both from within the sport and from the real world.

Prior to the book overview, it is important at this time to offer some clarification. Namely, this book is written for male and female coaches, so the use of "he" is used throughout the book to simply keep the reading uniform and consistent. This by no means indicates a sexist overtone to the writing of this text. Moreover, this book is primarily written for coaches and players of the indoor game, but the mental-training principles listed in the book could easily be applied to the beach game.

This book is divided into three general sections. Section I, consisting of Chapters 1 through 4, describes the many intricacies behind performance excellence—mainly, talent, skill, mechanics, and automatic execution. Talent is something you are born with, while skill encompasses movement patterns, physical elements, and the skills of being mentally and emotionally tough. Technical mechanics encapsulate the specific aspects of each task, like the many aspects to setting a "quick." Mental and emotional toughness is defined as the ability to remain focused, energized, and confident in good times and in pressure situations. Mental mechanics, although similar to mental toughness, specifically refers to the mental processes involved with the execution of the task, mainly, the automaticity of skill execution. The final chapter in this section details the importance of the mind-body connection for sport performance. Specifically, offensive and defensive mental skills are addressed, along with a questionnaire that athletes could complete to determine their mental skill strengths and weaknesses.

Section II, Chapters 5–7, addresses the numerous performance barriers that can interfere with a player or team fulfilling their talent and skill potential. These barriers include the physical, the technical and strategic, the numerous team barriers, and the mental and inspirational blocks. This section concludes with a comprehensive explanation of how these barriers interfere with both technical and mental mechanical execution of setting, blocking, swinging, passing, and making and breaking plays.

Section III, Chapters 8–12, shows coaches and players how to successfully overcome these performance barriers so natural talent, skills, and mechanics can dominate. Navigating players through the endless barrage of performance barriers will help to "free their minds" from "baggage" and mental interference so they can focus instead on automatically and consistently performing the plays they have practiced over and over. Mental "skills and drills" can sometimes be thought of as being too "psychological" and thus beyond the scope of what coaches know. This section details the many ways that coaches already utilize mental-skills training strategies in their everyday coaching.

The last section, Section IV, includes Chapters 13 and 14. These chapters describe strategies for coaches and players to improve upon the quality of player and team practice. Since the practice setting is where the majority of the learning takes place, there is a direct relationship between the quality of practice and the quality of play on the game court. A quality training model is detailed in this section, highlighted by a questionnaire that players can complete to gain greater insight into their practice strengths and weaknesses. The final chapter details important elements to being the most effective coach, especially at the youth level, based upon research and presentations conducted on coach effectiveness by the author.

Just as there are many ways of teaching the back row attack, many methods exist for improving mental toughness. Mental training goes far beyond just "thinking positive," playing "relaxed," or simply utilizing "imagery" before playing. Mastering the technical skills needed to successfully perform at the highest levels of play requires quality practice, unwavering commitment, and a drive to get better. The same holds true for wanting to be a more complete player through improving mental toughness. Players must be committed to not only increase their awareness skills (what is working versus what isn't), but also be mindful of the many performance barriers that could be interfering with their play (the "why" things are not going well). The final step is to be able to respond quickly to overcome the particular barrier via specific mental toughness techniques. It cannot be stated enough that continual practice of the mental toughness training strategies detailed throughout this book is critical for any lasting effect.

The primary objective of this book is to assist players, coaches, and teams to maximize their performance potential via a greater appreciation of the "intangibles," namely the mental, emotional, and inspirational aspects inside every performer. Demystifying sport psychology is another objective because there are still so many coaches and athletes out there who do not feel that the mental aspects of their games are important, and that sport psychology principles are "hokey" or simply do not apply to them. In this book, there are many examples of ways that coaches actually utilize sport psychology principles in their everyday coaching practices, like pep talks, use of video, and imagery. It is very important for coaches to see that sport psychology can be used to enhance their own coaching practices as well as performance enhancement for players and teams.

The practical tips presented throughout this book are "tried and true," as they say. The author has been blessed to have worked with outstanding players and coaches from the youth, collegiate, professional, and Olympic levels, who so generously shared their years of playing and coaching experiences. This book is primarily a collection of these "nuggets" of wisdom and practical tools.

Applying these "nuggets" will enable each player to perform on all cylinders, allowing natural ability, talent, and learned skills and mechanics to come through on demand, especially when it is most needed, such as in the big rivalry game, state or club championship, or national championship match!

Section I:
Components of Toughness

1

Going Beyond the X's and O's: Talent, Skill, Toughness, and Mechanics

Talent, skill, toughness, and mechanics—words such as these are used in everyday conversations to evaluate the performances of both players and teams. But what do these terms really mean? Collectively, they actually represent the determining factors of athletic and team performance potential. Figure 1-1 depicts these important components of athletic potential. Although talent is something that is "given" to athletes, skill, mental toughness, and mechanics are elements that can be improved upon through good coaching and diligent practice.

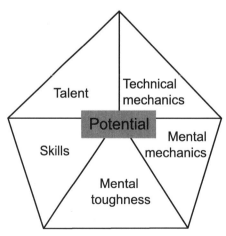

Figure 1-1. Aspects of athletic potential

The first component of athletic potential is *talent*, which is composed of a player's genetic potential—basically what his parents have so generously given him. Whether these "gifts" are welcomed or not, they are relatively stable and beyond a player's immediate control. Talent in certain domains may not be evident at an early age (thus, the use of the term "relatively" in the previous sentence), so coaches and parents need to be careful not to jump to conclusions about future success based upon what is observed early on. As a side note, Chapter 14 details some developmental considerations for coaches who work with younger players, including appropriate expectations and talent identification issues.

Talent is affected by genetic traits such as height, weight, athleticism, speed, coordination, quickness, flexibility, agility, spatial orientation, and body type. A researcher who has studied talent identification revealed several acronyms used by professional clubs that represent specific criteria used to assess athletic potential (Kluka, 2004). TIPS stands for technique, intelligence, personality, and speed; TABS refers to technique, attitude, balance, and speed; and SUPS refers to speed, understanding, personality, and skill. It is interesting to note that the evaluative criteria used by professional clubs include physical, mental, technical, and tactical attributes—all believed to be important for future success. Kluka (2004) explained that there has been a shift among researchers from talent detection (discovery of potential performers) to talent identification, guidance, and development (i.e., putting the

Courtesy of USC Sports Information

Figure 1-2. Sound technical mechanics takes the synergy of numerous processes

emphasis on the learning environment and quality of instruction instead of simply identifying critical attributes).

Although a particular athlete may not have been given all of the physical "gifts" of a great athlete—like a great pair of hands—this does not mean that he is limited in any way. All it means is that accomplishing great things on the court will not be as easy as it is for those who are "gifted" genetically. It is in such cases that qualities such as a player's work rate, drive, commitment, and toughness play an integral role.

The next component is *skill*, which, unlike the "gift" of athletic talent, players have total control over. Skills are learned, and can be constantly improved upon and enhanced. Basic movement patterns like jumping, running, backpedaling, sprinting, diving, rolling, and sidestepping are all skills. Specific physical and visual motor skills include setting, passing, blocking, swinging, seeing gaps and seams in blocking coverages and defenses, and reacting to ever-changing situations.

Another major component of an athlete's arsenal is *technical mechanics*. Performing a task, like executing a blocking scheme perfectly, takes the synergy of numerous components that, when combined, form a motor sequence or pattern in the mind and muscles. Using the setter as an example, these components, referred to as the technical mechanics of the task, include:
- The locomotor sequence of the task, which includes the necessary footwork for the prescribed situation, like setting off of the back foot, jump sets, or back sets.
- Postural movements, such as the proper preparation of the hands prior to setting from all types of body and court positions, such as setting balls out of the net, setting off of bad passes, and back court sets.
- The manipulation component, which includes finger spacing, touch, and appropriate contact point, like the "high point," and good hand absorption.
- Decision-making, which involves the type of set needed (low to high set, fast to slow set), delivery speed, location, amount of spin, and trajectory.
- Sensory or perceptual elements, which include the interpretation of situation-specific cues that direct the decisions to be made, including the position of the opponent's middle blockers, for example. Spatial orientation is important for knowing where the opponents are positioned at all times.
- Conceptual elements of the setting task, which include what the setter is focusing on prior to skill execution, in terms of the play call, using hot hitters, exploiting an opponent's weakness, and the focus of his attention prior to and during the execution (too narrow a focus, too broad, or just right).

While the prerequisite movement, physical, and visual motor skills are very important, two additional skills are needed for consistent, optimal play—*mental* and *emotional toughness*. These skills are widely recognized as being important to top performance, yet are so often ignored during practice sessions. It is often said that at the higher levels of sport, physical talent and technical skill are somewhat even among the players, and it is the level of mental toughness that differentiates the best from the rest.

Jim Loehr, a mental toughness expert, has defined mental and emotional toughness as being "...the ability to consistently perform toward the upper range of your talent and skill regardless of competitive circumstances" (2001, pg. 5). In other words, tough players can remain confident, focused, and energized with productive emotions in pressure-filled situations, such as being down early, having to hit poor sets, dealing with momentum shifts, or playing with injury.

Even in non-competitive situations, like during skill and drill work in practice, players should respond with intensity, focused attention, and a diligent goal-directed effort. Wanting to be mentally tough takes more than just talking about it, although it is a start. Mental toughness entails being in command over inner dialogue (referred to as self-talk), thoughts, feelings, and how one appraises situations. As you will learn, what athletes say, think, feel, and perceive can truly help or hurt their on-court performance. Mentally tough athletes think and talk tough, feel confident and energized, and perceive situations as being challenging rather than threatening. Ken Ravizza, former mental skills trainer for the Anaheim Angels and Los Angeles Dodgers, has stated that mental toughness is the ability to "be comfortable being uncomfortable." A mentally tough athlete is able to continue playing while not allowing the mind or an adversarial situation to interfere. When things get rough for this type of athlete, they are actually able to perform better because they do not allow adversity to get the best of them. Chapter 4 includes a mental toughness questionnaire called the Offensive and Defensive Mental Skills Survey, which will alert players to the specific mental-emotional toughness skills that they may be lacking.

Although mental toughness is usually applied to the individual player, teams can work toward a collective toughness. Chapter 10 addresses ways of not only improving team unity and cohesion, but also how to help teams accept a common vision and identity.

The final component of athletic potential is *mental mechanics*. Each player on the court performs different skill tasks depending upon their position and their specific assignment on each play. The specific motor programs needed to execute these different tasks are developed over time through quality, repetitive training during practice. For players to take what they do repeatedly in practice onto the game court, each mechanical component must be taught, practiced, evaluated, and practiced over and over again. Once players begin to master the nuances of each technical skill, game situations and game simulations should then be introduced. Incorporating technical mechanics into your everyday teaching will better prepare players for quality execution in practice and at game time. The next step is for players to be able to execute these motor programs automatically, without having to think about what to do and how to do it. This automatic processing, or mental mechanics, is a major determinant of optimal, consistent play. That is why this automatic execution should be the goal of any performer.

Each player's faith in his own talent, skills, mental toughness, and quality training is at the core of automatic performance and thus, is the central theme of this book. Chapter 2 goes into greater detail on how technical and mental mechanics are linked and how to sharpen them to improve execution and automaticity of action.

Courtesy of USC Sports Information

Figure 1-3. Playing automatically entails letting go of conscious control and just going for it!

Chapter Summary

- Athletic potential consists of numerous determining variables, including talent, skill components, and technical and mental mechanics.
- Two very important skills that can and should be improved upon and practiced are mental and emotional toughness.
- Mental and emotional toughness are defined as the ability to be resilient, confident, focused, and energized in times of pressure and adversity.
- Coaching the technical mechanics of a skill involves more than just teaching the physical components (e.g., footwork, preparation movements, and manipulation). Being able to base decisions on the interpretation of situation-specific cues and then executing the skills based upon this information are critical ingredients to effective execution practices.
- Mental mechanics is the ability of athletes to be able to execute the technical mechanics of a task without overthinking or allowing distractions to interfere.

2

Technical and Mental Mechanics: Automatic Processing

When players are first learning how to pass, hit, serve, dig, and set, they must concentrate on all the little details, beginning with the demonstration of the desired skill, the critical instruction phrases from the coach, and then the continual practice reps. After each correction, this process is repeated over and over. In the beginning, they can only do one skill aspect at a time. As they progress, a lot of conscious thinking is still being conducted, and yet common mistakes dwindle. Once players begin to master the particular technical mechanics of the skill, they begin to perform the skill sequence without having to think about each little piece—previously referred to as mental mechanics. Instead, a motor program has been developed and muscle memory leads the way. This ability to "free the mind" and not think through the skill during execution is a valuable aspect to consistent, optimal play.

An analogy often used to describe this process is teaching a teenager how to drive a car. The first time behind the wheel is scary for all parties involved. The driver is so narrowly focused, or has "tunnel vision," because he is trying to remember each step of the process, beginning with putting on the seat belt, turning the ignition, putting it into reverse, and looking in all directions before backing out. Once he gets out of the driveway, the real adventure begins. External stimuli, which include other cars, pedestrians, crossings, lights, and signs, are in need of immediate and constant attention, not to mention the continual checks of car speed and looking at the mirrors. Internal distractions are also present, including fears and anxieties about driving a car

Figure 2-1. Learning skills for the first time entails conscious thought and lots of practice.

Courtesy of Ralf's Photography/SCVC

for the first time. But after numerous trials, the countless steps and potential distractions seem to disappear, as the new driver is suddenly able to keep the car on the road while selecting the next tune on the CD player or having a conversation with passengers without really thinking. This example illustrates how automatic processing occurs due to the synergy between physical, technical, and mental processes that result through continual, quality practice.

In both of these examples, the performer, whether it be a beginning player or a beginning driver, had to think through each of their specific actions to get the job done. Yet once they began to learn the necessary skills, the body and mind just take over all of the execution processes, signifying efficient technical mechanics, and no longer require continual focus, indicating sound mental mechanics.

Keep in mind that even top-level athletes go through this learning process whenever there is a change made to their technical mechanics. In some situations, especially when a player is struggling through a performance slump, changes are made to an already established mechanical program. As a side note, this is usually not the recommended method to reverse the deleterious effects of a performance slump. In most cases, making changes will only lead to more mechanical problems, since these changes are usually not practiced as extensively as needed. For example, when an otherwise consistent skill, like serving, hitting, or passing, all of a sudden becomes inconsistent, it could be caused by a physical, mental, or emotional barrier, rather than a technical problem. Section II details numerous performance barriers that could initially cause, or assist in continuing, performance slumps.

To fully integrate even the most minute change, the athlete must focus intently on each piece of the process, much like he had to do when just starting out. Yet when these slight adjustments are made, mistakes will become an important part of the process, and should not be fretted over in the short-term. Changes to skill execution must be made only when sufficient practice time exists to incorporate these alterations. With continual quality practice, changes are integrated and the desired performance results occur. Tiger Woods, arguably the best golfer in the world, has made significant changes to his swing throughout the years, even after winning his first Masters. With each change came hours and hours of focused practice in an attempt to revise an already established and successfully consistent motor program. The great ones, like Roger Clemens, Wayne Gretzky, Brett Favre, Karch Kiraly, Holly McPeak, and Paula Weishoff, are always looking to achieve another level of greatness. Making changes like these is risky for most, because of the time needed to institute change. Even the great ones must devote practice time towards integrating the new elements before automatic processing can be assured.

"You can't miss nor can you wait to get to the next green. Pretty soon you're on autopilot, playing by instinct and feel. That's as close to finding your own game as you can get. Sometimes we think too much instead of trusting that inner voice that says you can do it."
—Tiger Woods, Four-time Masters Winner (2001, p. 259)

Automatic processing can be quite unstable due to many factors that act to sabotage the process. Section II details the voluminous barriers that interfere with automatic execution. The strength of an athlete's mental toughness and mental mechanics is tested when confronted with these performance barriers. Performers who are able to successfully defend themselves against the damaging effects of performance barriers will be much more consistent in pressure-packed, game situations than those who are "beginners" in terms of their mental toughness and mental mechanics.

One such performance barrier is attentional capacity. How much an athlete can focus on at one time is actually quite limited, especially in the presence of hundreds of potential visual and auditory distractions. Yet among the stimuli bombarding the player, some are needed to effectively execute the next play. Blockers look for key cues at the net to decide their blocking schemes and setters look for cues from the opposing blockers to set quick reads on what set and play to run. The same can be said about other positional players who utilize cues from the environment to get their respective jobs done. Proficiency at focusing in this manner entails not only knowing what cues to attend to, but also being able to let go of "clutter" that may interfere with this processing. An entire array of performance barriers is addressed in Section II.

How does a player work to improve upon technical and mental mechanics so "clutter" of this kind does not interfere with performance? The answer lies in knowing how to maximize the mind-body connection, which is at the core of the sport psychology principles presented throughout this book. Maximizing the connection between the mind, which encompasses our thoughts, self-talk, attitudes, feelings, motives, and perceptions, and our *body*, which consists of physical sensations, emotional reactions, technical proficiency, and physical performances, entails conscious awareness of how this connection works. Chapter 3 provides the information necessary to enhance awareness of how the mind can help, yet also hurt, athletic performance. An applied model will then be presented to describe what coaches and players can do to utilize this mind-body connection to their advantage and maximize performance.

Chapter Summary

- Automatic processing results when athletes can let go of conscious thoughts and allow their skills, talent, and practice to take over.
- Whenever experienced players make even the most subtle changes to an established technical skill they should expect some delay in playing to their former level because of the relearning process. Performance in practice will include some miscues until the new skill component(s) become automatic, which takes continual quality practice and game-simulated practice.
- Performance barriers can sabotage a player's automatic execution of even the most well-learned skills.
- Being more aware of how the mind and body works to help and hurt athletic performances is a critical lesson to learn if optimal, consistent performance is a goal.

3

The Mind-Body Connection: Maximizing the Capacity for Excellence

"If you as a coach are good at analyzing and adjusting the mental and emotional state of your team, then you will win many matches against coaches who don't understand it."
—Pete Waite, Volleyball Coach, Wisconsin (2002, p. 306)

"Nowhere is it more abundantly clear than in competitive sports that everything is interconnected. What you think, how you act, what you eat, how much you sleep, your fighting spirit, your fitness, your passion for life are all intimately connected."
—Jim Loehr, Ed.D., Mental Skills Trainer (Braden, 2002, p. 33)

"You get out what you put in ... you can't be half in and half out. Coaches don't say the game is 90% mental for the hell of it."
—Mike Stoops, Head Football Coach, Arizona (Dufresne, 2004, p. D12)

These quotes typify what some coaches and players believe about the application of mental-skills training to their chosen sport. How common is it to hear or read in interviews with coaches and players about mental issues contributing to wins or losses?

Sound bites such as "we just weren't in it tonight," "we didn't do the little things," or even "we started out too flat and couldn't climb out of the hole we dug because of it," are quite common. Conversely, coaches also cite mental or team factors after wins, including "we played as a team tonight," "we stayed positive despite some early troubles," or "we stayed focused on the game plan and executed."

Despite the growth of the sport psychology field in the last decade, and the increase in the number of teams and athletes who utilize sport psychology consultants, some misconceptions still exist regarding the mental aspects of sport. Chapter 11 describes the many ways that coaches and players already apply sport psychology principles to their game. Teaching and practicing the mental side of volleyball can be integrated into everyday coaching practices, especially if coaches realize that they are already doing it.

The following questions bring up specific situations that provide more evidence on how the mind and body link affects volleyball performance.

- Does it appear that sometimes players "forget" how to execute well-learned skills and plays?
- How often do players fall short of fulfilling their performance potential?
- How often do players talk negatively about themselves before, during, or after play?
- Does the team consider itself to be a slow-starting team? How about a come-from-behind team?
- Do players play well after making mistakes?
- Do players play poorly on the road?
- Do they play well under pressure?
- How many players are good practice players but fall short when it comes to game-time?
- Does it appear that sometimes players quit trying after experiencing adversity?
- Do players know what specific areas to their games are strengths and which areas are in need of improvement?

These questions bring to the forefront the important connections between the mind and the body. The questions each refer to one of 10 specific mind-body connections. How many of these scenarios play themselves out throughout the course of a season with your team or players?

• *Does it appear that players sometimes forget how to run well-learned plays?* An excess of anxiety can affect concentration, memory, and the execution of well-learned skills. Anxiety can also create physical tension or increase mental interference, and in turn affect confidence levels and ultimately performance.

Courtesy of Bradley Cole

Figure 3-1. The mental aspects of volleyball are acknowledged yet seldom practiced.

• *How often do players fall short of fulfilling their potential?* In what specific areas do players and teams fall short? The topic of expanding upon player capacities for performance excellence is detailed later in this chapter.

• *How often do players talk negatively about themselves?* Negative self-talk directly and indirectly affects confidence, motivation, competitive focus, anxiety, and performance.

• *Do players on the team consider themselves to be slow starters?* The use of one-trial generalizations, or the labeling of strengths or weaknesses based upon one outcome, is a troublesome practice. For example, if a team begins a game by giving up an early run of points but then win in the end, they may declare to others that they are "slow starters." This can set into motion a "self-fulfilling prophecy" whereby this team always starts out slowly, leaving to chance the ability to pull out the victory on a consistent basis. Using the self-fulfilling prophecy in a productive way is definitely recommended, such as the belief that the team is a fast starting one, or that a team is able to finish off opponents. More is mentioned of the self-fulfilling prophecy in Chapter 12.

- *Do players play well after making mistakes?* Most players who are not able to let go of mistakes will continue making the same mistakes. It is like playing with a "monkey on your back." The more mistakes that are allowed to pile on, the bigger the burden becomes. If players have not prepared for potential setbacks, via refocusing or coping routines, they will continue to allow mistakes to knock them off of their games.

- *Do players play poorly on the road?* Finding ways to focus on the job at hand will often lead to a "silencing of the crowd" through solid play and execution, thereby drawing players' attention away from a hostile environment.

- *Do they play well under pressure?* Helping players realize what they do and do not have control over can help them focus on what needs to be done presently, regardless of the situation and their own anxiety levels.

- *How many players are good practice players but fall short when it comes to game-time?* Great practice players lose something when it comes to game-time performance. Fears and anxieties take center stage, mixed with an inability to cope with these performance barriers. Talent and skill will forever be hindered if these barriers are not overcome.

- *Does it appear that players quit after experiencing adversity?* Adversity, whether it comes in the form of being down big early or late, losing a key starter, or bad officiating calls, must be overcome. Having organized plans to deal with potential adversity is one method; another is to be in better control of emotional reactions to adversity.

- *Do players know their strengths and weaknesses?* Players who are not aware of what does and does not work for them tend to "go through the motions" in practice since they do not have adequate direction regarding the route to consistent, optimal performance.

These questions accentuate the importance of how players think and talk to themselves prior to, during, and after performing, as well as the impact these thoughts and self-dialogue have on actions, physical sensations (tension, relaxation), behaviors, feelings, and ultimately performance. Additionally, how players emotionally react to pressure situations and adversity can either adversely affect or improve upon performance.

> *"Sometimes you can find yourself falling off track and going to the negative side of things...you just have to keep a positive attitude about everything."*
> —Fred Taylor, Running Back, Jacksonville Jaguars (NFL)
> (Stellino, 2002, p. D10)

Although the previous questions are asked primarily to assess weaknesses that some players or teams may have with the interconnection between the mind and body, these same questions can also highlight strengths. Players who transfer the work done on the practice field to the game usually do not get rattled under pressure or adversity, and continue to work hard under duress. This success is the result of solid mental and emotional toughness and sound mental mechanics. As discussed in Chapter 1, some players inherit the talent necessary for optimal play, including physical, technical, and mental skills, while others have to work extremely hard to maximize the gifts they have been given.

Very few players, however, especially at the middle school, high school, and college levels, truly have *complete* games. For this reason, most teams (or players) employ coaches of all types to help players improve upon all areas of their game and progress toward becoming complete players. These coaches can range from positional, strength, speed, and flexibility coaches, to nutrition experts and even dance teachers to help players improve agility and footwork. Occasionally, a sport psychologist is hired to speak to the team, albeit only one or two times during a season. Although the use of specialists such as these can be quite beneficial, coaches can help each one of their athletes become complete players by coaching not just the physical and technical aspects of volleyball, but the mental game as well—the missing link in some cases during their everyday practices.

An applied model that can be employed by coaches at all competitive levels to help expand upon their players' overall games, or capacities, is shown in Figure 3-2. As indicated, the pyramid-shaped model represents the seven categories critical to optimal performance. The lower sections of the pyramid represent those areas that are trained on a regular basis, are deemed most important by coaches, and are easier to "fix." The areas toward the top of the pyramid represent those aspects that are trained less frequently and are more difficult to master, especially without adequate information and strategies. Coaches have put a heavy emphasis on helping athletes maximize their physical, technical, and strategic abilities.

Although some coaches do emphasize the importance of team unity and effectiveness, an important challenge for coaches is to assist players in expanding their *mental, emotional,* and *inspirational* capacities. Maximizing performance capacities will enable players to play closer to their full potential by sharpening their skills and

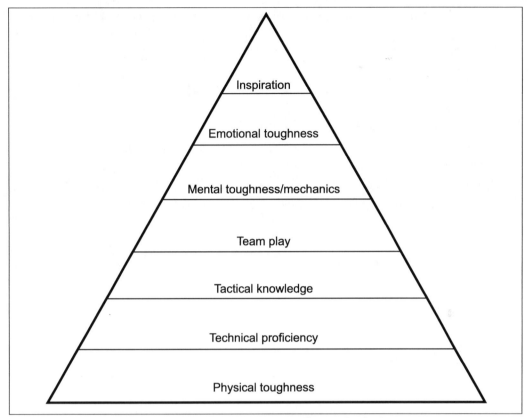

Figure 3-2. Expanding player capacities for more complete individual games

mechanical strengths while improving upon their weaker areas. Before this improvement can be made, players must become aware of their strengths and weaknesses.

> *"The pursuit of excellence begins with getting to know your own patterns. This is simply a process of becoming more aware of your own capacities, strengths, and weaknesses. It also means becoming more aware of what you really want, as opposed to what others want of you."*
> —Terry Orlick, Ph.D., Mental Skills Trainer (2000, p. 79)

Performance capacities are defined by a list of qualities that can be seen by coaches and players alike. Players and teams who show these particular qualities are close to maximizing their capacity in the specified area. For example, a player who is as strong and fit as he can be is maximizing his physical capacity, and thus, improves his chances for success. Players who are "complete" players can honestly report that they fulfill their capabilities across these seven performance areas. However, those players who do not employ these practices are falling shy of fulfilling their capacities, and lowering their chances at succeeding in practice and during matches.

Physical Capacity

Signs of maximizing physical capacity include:

- Players who maximally prepare their "machines" for practice and games by eating what they should and ensuring proper hydration
- Players who physically prepare in the off-season across all fitness principles: strength, endurance, speed, flexibility, aerobic endurance, power, agility, body composition, and vertical leaping ability
- Players who provide themselves with adequate rest, recovery, and stretching between practice and games
- Players who do not allow fatigue to inhibit their play

"Volleyball is an extremely difficult sport to prepare for physically. Our sport is neither aerobic nor purely anaerobic; it requires an unusual combination of the two energy systems."
—Doug Beal, Head Coach, US National Team (2002, p. 50)

Conditioning and fitness are two parts of a player's performance that are totally within his control. Players can be as fit as they want to be; they just need to put in the necessary time and the effort. Chapter 5 details the many physical barriers that could limit players from expanding their physical toughness capacities, and Chapter 8 describes how players and coaches can effectively combat these barriers.

Technical Capacity

Signs of maximizing technical capacity include:

- Players who know what specific technical skills need improving and actively train these areas at game speed
- Players who practice on their own, and ask for help from coaches, to improve particular technical aspects
- Players who focus on the mechanical aspects of the skill when learning something new, or when adding a new "wrinkle" to a previously learned skill
- Players who are consistent with their positional skills

Chapter 1 lists the many technical mechanics to a skill, including the locomotor sequencing and manipulation components, as well as the perceptual and conceptual elements that should be included in everyday teaching and subsequent repetition training. Players who are able to pinpoint, on their own, the specific mechanical areas that went awry after mistakes or poor execution will be better able to make necessary corrections on the court during the flow of play and practice. Empowering athletes with this type of awareness, called self-regulation in the sport psychology literature, can be invaluable to a player's development.

Tactical Capacity

Signs of maximizing tactical capacity include:
- Players who know all the necessary plays and reads that make up their specific assignments, both offensive (e.g., back row attack, attack line or angle, quick setting) and defensive (e.g., serve receive, blocking schemes, defending the quick set and dump).
- Players who internalize what they see from game tape and the scouting reports regarding their positions and roles
- Players who also know some of what their teammates are doing, or should be doing in certain cases

Jacob Rogers, a former tackle on the two-time national champion USC football team, was quoted in a *Los Angeles Times* article (September 24, 2003) as saying: "My dad always taught me to learn what everyone around you is supposed to do, because when you get into game time, situations happen and you might have to help somebody out." True students of the game adopt these tactical qualities and attempt to maximize their tactical knowledge and applications. Doug Beal, Olympic men's volleyball coach, has emphasized the tactical strategies for volleyball's most important position, the setter: "If the setter can accomplish the good set, then the role expands to becoming a smart setter. The smart setter will match a team's strategies to opponents' weaknesses, will feed the hot attacker, will take advantage of what the offense does best, and will effectively carry out the thoughts and plans of the coach" (2004, p. 80).

Team Capacity

Signs of maximizing team capacity include:
- Players who are willing to sacrifice individual acclaim for team pursuits
- Players who hold themselves accountable for their behaviors and actions
- Teams that are committed to the same goals and accept what it will take to get there
- Team members who know and accept their roles
- Players who help to motivate and inspire their teammates to get better
- Players who are able to communicate with their coaches and teammates

Courtesy of Ralf's Photography/SCVC

Figure 3-3. Setters become "smart" setters by expanding their performing capacities.

- Teams who "buy into" the coaches' system and help each other adhere to the accompanying standards

Most coaches know what the "disease of me" is and how it can ruin a team's pursuit of excellence. Pat Riley, former Laker "Showtime" coach and former Miami Heat coach, originally coined this phrase in his 1993 book. Are your players willing to sacrifice the "me" for the "we"? Do you have players who are more about their individual numbers and accomplishments than the collective efforts of the team? Without an honest commitment to the team ethic, teams will fail to play up to their expectations and potential.

Players need to make a conscious effort at being not only "coachable" but good team players. "Putting the team first" is a common value coaches try to impress upon their players, but how many players actually practice this on a daily basis? Being a team player is a skill which must be practiced, just like any technical or mental skill. Chapter 10 discusses team-building practices, which primarily consist of activities for players to improve upon their ability of putting the team first.

Mental Capacity

"Mental toughness is many things and rather difficult to explain. Its qualities are sacrifice and self-denial. Also, most importantly, it is combined with a perfectly disciplined will that refuses to give in. It's a state of mind—you could call it character in action."
—Vince Lombardi, Hall of Fame Football Coach
(Dorfman, 2003, p. 165)

Character in action—signs of maximizing mental capacity include:

- Players who look to the mental side of their games to gain an edge over their opponents via setting goals, imagining success, using intensity-control techniques, putting in quality practice sessions, contributing in putting the team first, and communicating with coaches and teammates
- Players who are consistently able to remain confident regardless of how they, or their team, are performing
- Players who are consistently able to prepare and ready themselves to play against any opponent, and thus, are not as likely to play "down" to the level of competition
- Players who remain focused on their specific roles for the upcoming play rather than being distracted by past mistakes or worries about what the next play will bring
- Players who are successfully able to not only let go of mistakes but also to learn from them and ready themselves for the next serve
- Players who are able to motivate themselves to play their "A" games regardless of the opponent, as well as being able to consistently give their best efforts throughout their practice sessions
- Players who are able to consistently prepare and ready themselves to practice and play to their maximum potential, which includes dealing with their confidence, anxiety, fears, worries, tension, and negative moods
- Players who are consistently able to "let go" of conscious control over their mechanics and allow themselves to trust their skills and simply "go for it," rather than thinking their way through execution

Mental toughness was defined earlier as the ability to remain confident, focused, energized, and composed in all types of performance situations, especially pressure situations. Being able to rise to the occasion in big games is tantamount to being a top competitor, but so is bringing one's level of motivation, effort, and execution up during a tedious drill, doing basic reps of a needed skill, or finding energy during the second hour of practice. Players who are able to rise to all of these occasions are truly mentally tough competitors and are players coaches love to coach.

Courtesy of USC Sports Information

Figure 3-4. Players like Keao Burdine, a two-time championship final MVP from USC, know a thing or two about rising to the occasion in big matches.

Those athletes who are mentally tough are easy to spot because they get the ball when big plays need to be made. These players are leading the team via their words and actions. Most players at the higher levels of the game are so into themselves and their own games that it shows something special when players are able to take care of themselves yet also offer to help their team excel to their utmost of its capabilities. They also perform consistently well regardless of what is going on around them. A consistent competitor who knows a thing or two about mental toughness is Tiger Woods. In his book, *How I Play Golf*, he detailed the following five "building blocks to mental toughness" (2001, p. 258-9):

- Learn from the positive and negatives from your performances.
- Take ownership of your mistakes—you are the one who is responsible for them.
- Never repeat mistakes.
- Be able to turn negatives into positives.
- After tough outings, don't beat yourself up too much because plenty of people will do it for you.

No real secrets here, but the difference between Tiger and the rest of the field is that he actually does these things and does not simply read them.

Emotional Capacity

Signs of maximizing emotional capacity include:
- Players who are consistently able to deal well with unexpected events, such as lineup changes due to injuries or performance slumps, broken plays, a change in formations, and routine alterations, such as arriving late to the game due to transportation problems or inclement weather
- Players who are able to cope with frustration over making mistakes, poor play, and other adversities, such as coaches' decisions, teammates' actions, or officials' calls
- Players who are able to remain strong and resilient when fatigued or nursing minor aches and pains
- Players who are able to free their minds of fears and anxieties and control their emotions so they can play with all of their talents and skills
- Players and teams who have the ability to consistently deal with momentum changes. Volleyball, unlike other sports, is predicated on these momentum swings. Teams that are able to sustain momentum when they have it, and regain it when it is lost, have the best chance at succeeding.

Operating to one's fullest emotional capacity entails the ability to take risks and not fear the potential negative consequences of these risks. Players who lack emotional toughness are fearful of these consequences, primarily the fear of it being discovered that they are not good players. This lack of internal confidence is quite common, even among those players who "talk" great games and are very boastful of their playing. Talking themselves up in this fashion helps keep the "critics" at bay, while protecting their deflated confidence and keeping these insecurities beneath the surface. Methods players can use to improve their internal confidence are addressed throughout this book, but especially in Chapter 12.

Players who are emotionally tough play all-out and never worry about what others are thinking or saying about them or their play. These players do not "handicap" themselves by coming up with excuses prior to playing, such as "I'm not feeling my best today," "My ankle is still a little tender," "I'm still getting over that cold," or "I don't play well in this arena." If a less emotionally tough player fails to dominate, and their "critics" begin thinking that the player is not a *player*, these excuses can be used as a shield to deflect the criticism and protect his image as being a top-notch player.

Inspirational Capacity

Signs of maximizing inspirational capacity include:
- Players who truly *love* playing volleyball and their specific positions
- Players who are consistently "into it" and are doing all that is necessary to improve upon their individual play
- Players who willingly make sacrifice of their time, their bodies, and their social activities for the sake of their individual pursuit
- Players who know exactly why they play volleyball and what they plan on accomplishing in the sport
- Players who find inspiration from a multitude of sources, including their own maximal efforts, teammates, coaches, and other outside sources, which could include other players, past coaches and teammates, and news articles, to name a few

"Personal excellence is largely a question of believing in your own capacities and fully committing yourself to your own development."
—Terry Orlick, Ph.D., Mental Skill Trainer (2000, p. 40)

In a *Los Angeles Times* article (July 2003) Eric Crouch, former Nebraska quarterback and 2001 Heisman Trophy winner, decided to quit pro football after stints with St. Louis and Green Bay. He stated that "I just couldn't get excited about it. I couldn't be passionate about it." It seemed as though Eric Crouch lost his inspiration to play. How many players on your team appear to have lost their inspiration to play and improve? Players who simply go through the motions in practice are those who lose sight of their goals and aspirations, and are not willing to commit their talents, abilities, and efforts. Much more will be discussed on what drives and inspires players in Chapter 6.

Figure 3-5. Having a more complete game can help players achieve great things.

Courtesy of Aiden Michael

The sections of the pyramid in Figure 3-2 are expanded upon in Figure 3-6, where each contains questions for players to answer that can help them gain a better awareness of their present capacity level. Before a player can operate to his maximal capacities, he must be aware of his current level and how far it may be from his top effort. If the majority of your players' responses to the questions are "no," this indicates that they are not working towards maximizing their specific capacities. Responses marked with a "yes" indicate progress toward becoming a complete player who plays a complete game.

Upon getting responses from each player and/or the team as a whole, individual/team meetings can be conducted to discuss specific areas that players need to commit to improving, as well as listing the players' areas of strengths. Coaches who take the time to talk about specific ways to maximize each athlete's capacities show the athletes how committed their coaches are in assisting them in their pursuit. The critical piece to this model is that your athletes and team are being asked the "right" questions—that is, questions that range across the seven different capacities.

Another exercise is to ask your players to determine the percentage of their mistakes due to each of these seven components. For example, if a player makes the majority of his mistakes because he is always a step too late or too slow, he may need to improve upon his first-step speed and agility (physical capacity). Those players who struggle with committing too many errors due to their frustration need some work on coping more effectively with their emotions (emotional capacity).

Another activity is to have players brainstorm why they have not been able to accomplish their most preferred goals due to barriers in these seven components. The players should then be asked to brainstorm some solutions to these barriers. A combination of the feedback gathered during these exercises can be an important foundation for subsequent team goal-setting sessions targeting solutions to common team problems and barriers.

Once players know what needs improvement, beginning with those areas that are easier to strengthen (physical, technical, and tactical), coaches and available support staff can offer their expertise in providing athletes with the means to bring about change via specific strategies and tools. Assistant coaches, strength coaches, trainers, and nutritionists can be valuable in improving physical toughness (strength and conditioning, recovery, and energization), whereas a sport psychology consultant can help strengthen team, mental, emotional, and inspirational toughness.

Since the coaching staff knows the players best, their input and suggestions will be paramount, along with their continual follow-up and feedback to the athlete and team as a whole. Although the use of sport psychology consultants can be very valuable

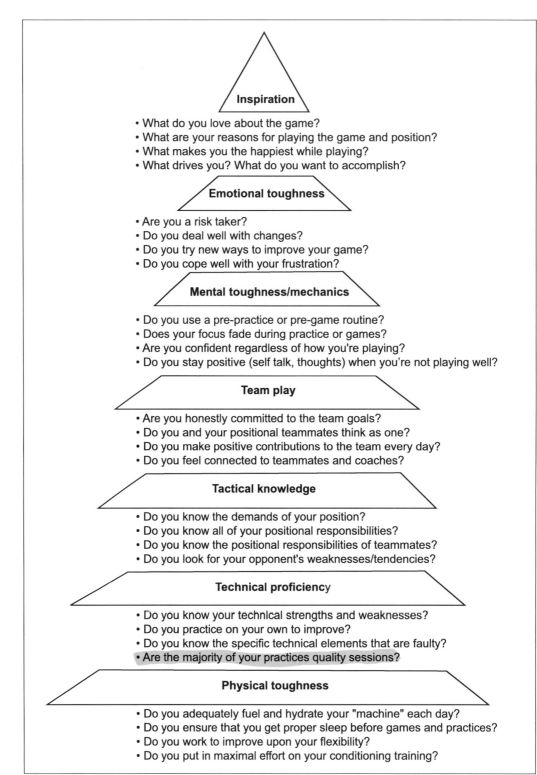

Inspiration
- What do you love about the game?
- What are your reasons for playing the game and position?
- What makes you the happiest while playing?
- What drives you? What do you want to accomplish?

Emotional toughness
- Are you a risk taker?
- Do you deal well with changes?
- Do you try new ways to improve your game?
- Do you cope well with your frustration?

Mental toughness/mechanics
- Do you use a pre-practice or pre-game routine?
- Does your focus fade during practice or games?
- Are you confident regardless of how you're playing?
- Do you stay positive (self talk, thoughts) when you're not playing well?

Team play
- Are you honestly committed to the team goals?
- Do you and your positional teammates think as one?
- Do you make positive contributions to the team every day?
- Do you feel connected to teammates and coaches?

Tactical knowledge
- Do you know the demands of your position?
- Do you know all of your positional responsibilities?
- Do you know the positional responsibilities of teammates?
- Do you look for your opponent's weaknesses/tendencies?

Technical proficiency
- Do you know your technical strengths and weaknesses?
- Do you practice on your own to improve?
- Do you know the specific technical elements that are faulty?
- Are the majority of your practices quality sessions?

Physical toughness
- Do you adequately fuel and hydrate your "machine" each day?
- Do you ensure that you get proper sleep before games and practices?
- Do you work to improve upon your flexibility?
- Do you put in maximal effort on your conditioning training?

Figure 3-6. Capacity for excellence questions

(more valuable if you utilize an experienced, knowledgeable, professionally trained and certified consultant), some teams do not have the access or means to utilize these services. Coaches have utilized, and will continue to incorporate, sport psychology practices into their everyday coaching. Reading this book indicates a desire to improve upon your knowledge of sport psychology and coaching effectiveness. Chapter 11 details the many ways coaches incorporate mental skills training into their everyday coaching.

Section II delves deeper into the seven performance areas by specifying the numerous barriers players face when trying to perform to the utmost of their physical, technical, tactical, team, mental, emotional, and inspirational capacities. Section III discusses tested methods used to combat these voluminous barriers to consistent, optimal performance.

Chapter Summary

- How players think and talk to themselves prior to, during, and after games can be a great advantage or disadvantage, depending upon the content of these cognitions (i.e., thoughts) and self-talk. For most, positive and productive thoughts and self-talk help performance, while negative thoughts and talk hinder top performance.
- For players to have "complete" games, coaches must teach not only the physical and technical aspects of volleyball but the mental game as well.
- Players who are "complete" players maximize their capacities across seven performance areas—physical, technical, tactical, team, mental, emotional, and inspirational.
- Before players can maximize their performance capacities, they must be aware of their current level and how far it is from their top effort.
- Although support staff can be valuable in helping players maximize their capacities to have more complete games, coaches are the critical pieces to the puzzle. Even the slightest knowledge of sport psychology principles and techniques will be of great assistance if passed along to players.

4

Offensive and Defensive Mental Toughness Skills

This book is meant to maximize players' performances through maximizing their capacities, which range from the physical to the inspirational. The previous chapter defined these capacities, and subsequent chapters outline performance barriers that exist within each capacity and strategies that can be used to combat these barriers. This chapter delves deeper into evaluating strengths and weaknesses within the mental and emotional capacities, since these two areas are recognized as being important for consistent performance.

Sean McCann, director of sport psychology services at the United States Olympic Training Center, presented a model of mental skills that, in his words, "explains why athletes need mental skills and how they work in various sport situations...the model aids in making invisible mental skills become more visible" (2002, p. 11). This model is effective in presenting the importance of mental skills training as well as the application of training strategies to your players and fellow coaches.

The numerous mental skills are divided into two main categories: offensive and defensive. Because volleyball players appreciate the importance of both the defensive and offensive sides of the game, this model speaks with the jargon that players are used to hearing on a daily basis. Just as volleyball teams need to be solid on both sides of the ball to be successful, the same goes for athletes who are driven to succeed—they must have sharp offensive and defensive mental skills. McCann (2002) has defined offensive skills as those that allow players to perform to the top of their capacities and thus, dominate their performances. These skills include confidence, competitive focus, preparation, planning, readiness, visualization, and quality training. Defensive skills enable players to remain composed and resilient in the face of adversity. Skills such as the ability to refocus and recover from adversity, to control one's emotions and energy levels, and to "look" ready for the next play make up the defensive mental skills.

Offensive and Defensive Mental Skills Survey

Players may be strong in some of the mental skills but weak in others. The first step is to determine these strengths and weaknesses. The Offensive and Defensive Mental Skill Survey is a valuable tool in acquiring this information (Voight, 2004) (Figure 4-1).

This questionnaire is divided into numerous sections, each representing a key mental skill. These skills are defined by their influence on performance.

Offensive Mental Skills

- Confidence—the ability to trust their abilities and skills so they can perform automatically, without thought or hesitation
- Competitive focus—the ability to remain focused on the important performance cues necessary for successful execution
- Mental preparation—thinking in the present; not worrying over past mistakes or future performances. Also, with good mental preparations, players' thoughts and self-talk focuses on the process of improving, not on outcome or results.
- Quality of training—training that is process-focused, goal directed, and performed with maximal effort
- Use of imagery—the ability to see playing excellence, which can aid in confidence enhancement, preparation, and emotional control prior to and during play

Defensive Mental Skills

- Refocus—the ability to get back on track by focusing on game-related cues rather than on internal or external distractions
- Recovery—the ability to expeditiously deal with setbacks, allowing players to get back to their "ready," optimal state via thoughts and feelings
- Intensity control—the ability to control debilitating tension, thoughts, and self-talk to help stay on task and be process-focused
- Physical presentation—the ability to look stoic and confident regardless of the situation, such as being down early, in the midst of a slump, missed kills or shanked passes

Offensive and Defensive Mental Skills Survey

Please complete each sentence, and then respond by circling the number that corresponds with the most appropriate word.

KEY:

Never: 0   Very rarely: 1   Rarely: 2   Sometimes: 3   Often: 4   Very often: 5   Always: 6

	never					always	
1. I _____worry about making mistakes	0	1	2	3	4	5	6
2. I _____ have a very difficult time letting go of mistakes	0	1	2	3	4	5	6
3. I _____ bounce back quickly from setbacks	0	1	2	3	4	5	6
4. I _____ dwell on mistakes and "carry them" with me to the next play	0	1	2	3	4	5	6
5. I _____ consider myself a confident player	0	1	2	3	4	5	6
6. When I'm not playing well, I _____ get negative and get down on myself	0	1	2	3	4	5	6
7. On the court I _____ project a confident image regardless of the score	0	1	2	3	4	5	6
8. At critical times in games I _____ find myself thinking negatively	0	1	2	3	4	5	6
9. I _____find myself getting too nervous/anxious before/during games	0	1	2	3	4	5	6
10. I _____ do my best when the pressure is on	0	1	2	3	4	5	6
11. I _____find it difficult to get energized to play a lesser team	0	1	2	3	4	5	6
12. I _____ have poor focus when I have to make a critical play	0	1	2	3	4	5	6
13. I _____ get distracted during a match	0	1	2	3	4	5	6
14. I _____think too much while I play, instead of just playing	0	1	2	3	4	5	6
15. Poor officiating (calls), rowdy spectators, or opponent's behaviors _____ takes me off my game	0	1	2	3	4	5	6
16. I _____ get anxious (hope I don't choke) the crazier it gets in competition (weather, score, opponent behavior)	0	1	2	3	4	5	6
17. I am _____ a "slow starter," meaning that it takes me a while to get "into the rhythm" of the game	0	1	2	3	4	5	6
18. I _____ use a set pre-practice or pre-game routine to improve readiness	0	1	2	3	4	5	6

Figure 4-1. Offensive and Defensive Mental Skill Survey

19. My mind _____ wanders to end results and I have trouble focusing on the process of playing well   0   1   2   3   4   5   6

20. I _____ mentally picture the game plan and how I will play before practice and games   0   1   2   3   4   5   6

21. I _____ consistently train at a high level of intensity   0   1   2   3   4   5   6

22. I _____ find myself "going through the motions" in training sessions   0   1   2   3   4   5   6

23. I _____ focus well in practice/games when I have problems in my life outside of volleyball   0   1   2   3   4   5   6

24. When I practice, I _____ have a specific purpose or goal to accomplish   0   1   2   3   4   5   6

25. I _____ have a high-energy walk between games (especially when I am tired or frustrated with the past game)   0   1   2   3   4   5   6

26. Observers can _____ tell from my body language that I made a mistake or am playing poorly   0   1   2   3   4   5   6

27. My coaches and teammates can _____ tell by my body language and behaviors that I am frustrated and upset   0   1   2   3   4   5   6

28. If I am having difficulty with my play, I _____ take it out on my teammates or coaches   0   1   2   3   4   5   6

SCORING: To determine your mental skill strengths and weaknesses, use the following scoring method *by section*. REVERSE score the following items: 3, 5, 7, 10, 18, 20, 21, 23, 24, 25 as follows: 0=6; 1=5; 2=4; 3=3; 4=2; 5=1; 6=0

- If the score is *8 or fewer points*, this area is a mental strength.
- If the score is between *9 and 12 points*, you appear to have some difficulty with the particular mental skills; some work is recommended
- If the score is between *13 and 24 points*, you appear to have more serious difficulty with this particular mental skill; more work is definitely needed before your performance suffers more.

Defensive Mental Skills:

Section 1 = questions 1–4 deal with the ability to refocus and recover upon adversity (mistakes, setbacks).

Section 2 = questions 5–8 refer to confidence level.

Section 3 = questions 9–12 have to do with the ability to control levels of "intensity" (level of anxiety/muscle tension).

Offensive Mental Skills:

Section 4 = questions 13–16 refer to the ability to stay focused with distractions present.

Section 5 = questions 17–20 inquire about your ability to prepare physically/mentally for practice and matches.

Section 6 = questions 21–24 deal w/ the quality of training

Section 7 = questions 25–28 refer to your physical presentation when faced with adversity

Section 1=_____; Section 2=_____; Section 3=_____; Section 4=_____; Section 5=_____;
Section 6=_____; Section 7=_____.

• Emotional and energy control—the ability to remain composed under pressure; in practice settings or when playing against lesser opponents, the ability to get energized and motivated

Having each player complete the survey will provide both coaches and players with some important information. For example, if a player has higher scores (which on this survey represent weaknesses), this indicates deficiencies in a specific mental skill and this area should become a priority. If a player has high numbers on all the offensive mental skills, then this player is failing to dominant their performance, due to a lack of confidence and trust in his abilities and skills, while high scores on the defensive mental skills indicate problems with adversity and emotionality. Others may have weaknesses across both types of mental skills. Helping players interpret their scores on the Offensive and Defensive Mental Skill Survey and relate them to their present actions on the court can be a very valuable learning exercise for both coaches and players. Players can self-diagnose the issues leading to inconsistent performances, whereas their coaches will be better informed about the specific performance barriers limiting each player's performance potentials. The next two chapters will outline and detail these performance barriers.

Courtesy of AVP

Figure 4-2. Players who have sound offensive and defensive mental skills dominate their performances and remain focused under adversity.

Chapter Summary

- Two critical aspects of optimal performance so seldomly trained are the mental and emotional toughness skills.
- Mental and emotional skills can be organized into offensive and defensive skills.
- Offensive skills allow players to perform at the top of their games, while defensive skills enable players to remain composed in the face of adversity.
- Offensive mental skills include confidence, competitive focus, preparation and readiness, using productive images, and quality training.
- Defensive mental skills include refocus, recovery, intensity control, physical presentation, and emotional/energy control.

Section II:
Barriers and Breakdowns to
Performance Excellence

5

Barriers to Top Performance I: Physical, Technical, and Tactical Barriers

This chapter details the many physical, technical, and tactical barriers to optimizing performance, while Chapter 6 outlines the team, mental, emotional, and inspirational barriers. As mentioned in earlier chapters, when players master their technical and mental mechanics, as well as their mental toughness, automaticity of execution should result on a consistent basis. They should be better able to execute well-learned plays in pressure situations without thinking about the mechanical aspects of the chosen skill. The important word in the two previous sentences is "should." The practicality of teaching and training dictates that the more you practice something, the better it should be performed. But anyone involved in volleyball knows that this is not always the case. Why is that? Experts in the motor learning field have reported that physical, technical, and mental skills are susceptible to short-term conditions—fatigue, inadequate hydration and nutrition, mood swings, and external and internal distractions—all of which can result from the numerous variables that interfere with skill execution (Schmidt & Wrisberg, 2000).

These interference variables, referred to as *performance barriers*, can interfere with the maximizing of effort and execution (Figure 5-1). The performance barriers covered in this chapter include the following aspects of play: physical (e.g., not being fit enough), technical (e.g., weak at passing), and tactical (e.g., not understanding the play).

The first step in combating these barriers is to be aware of their existence and recognize when they directly or indirectly affect performance. What you may think is at

Technical-Tactical Barriers	Physical Barriers
• Role ambiguity	• Poor sleep habits
• Lack of understanding of the game plan	• Lack of proper recovery and hydrating
• Too much focus on execution of tactics	• Lack of proper fueling
• Game-speed training	• Training fatigue
• Visualization of roles and game plan	• Poor fitness conditioning

Figure 5-1. Common performance barriers

the root of a performance problem may not be the case at all. Teams and players who underperform, or are inconsistent, may be doing so because of "all of the above," barriers that range from the physical to the inspirational. First, determine whether the performance problem is primarily due to physical, technical, or tactical difficulties, because these are the easiest to "fix." For example, training smarter or improving technical execution via quality reps or by watching more video are methods players could perform to "fix" a problem. Another example is if a team is losing leads toward the ends of games. It may not be that they are losing confidence or the motivation to perform, signifying mental reasons. It may simply be that the players are physically fatigued due to the heat or being on the court for extended periods of time. When fatigued, skill execution can break down, causing ineffective plays and mental errors. This situation could also be due to players who are "on empty" in terms of inadequate hydration or nutrition.

Performance difficulties due to mental, team, emotional, or inspirational issues are much more complex, thus coaches should rule out physical, technical, or tactical reasons first. Another method of defeating these potential performance barriers is to challenge players to expand their individual capacities. Players must determine which areas of their performances are strengths and weaknesses, and they themselves must decide to strive toward maximizing their performance potential. Coaches are critical in this reflective process. The following sections detail the myriad of physical, technical, and tactical barriers that could be contributing to individual player and team not playing to potential or encountering other performance difficulties.

Physical Barriers

Beginning with the easiest of barriers to overcome, the physical barriers, athletes must be constantly working to improve upon all areas of game-related fitness. Although they may appear to be "little things,", inadequate nutrition and hydration can unquestionably interfere with top performance, as much as not having the physical skills necessary to compete. These two variables contribute greatly to the amount of energy that players bring to the practice and game courts. The basic fitness principles at the core of a player's execution potential include strength, power, aerobic fitness, anaerobic conditioning, agility, coordination, and speed-quickness. Although some of these attributes are "gifts," those not blessed with this type of natural talent can still maximize what they do have.

Most people know what can happen when the wrong type of fuel is added to our cars; the car may begin with some "pinging," then move on to "chugging," a decrease in pick-up and performance, and then finally undergo a complete shut-down of all operations. This often-used analogy paints a clear picture of what occurs in our bodies when poor nutrition is practiced on a consistent basis. Volleyball players, in their strength and conditioning work and on the practice and game courts, are in dire need of energy that can only be provided via the food and fluids ingested.

Carbohydrates are a prime energy source for high-intensity activity (e.g., conditioning, short bursts of speed and power), fats are necessary and provide energy for longer-duration activities (e.g., cardiovascular-type activities), and protein is a building block for tissue growth. Are players taking in adequate amounts of these prime nutrients as well as the essential vitamins and minerals, each of which carries out a different function in the body? Specific references are presented in Section III that offer greater detail about the relationship between sound nutrition and optimal sport performance.

The importance of keeping the body hydrated cannot be overemphasized. Ensuring that players are adequately hydrated before, during, and after competing should be a standard carried out daily. Insufficient hydration will not only have a deleterious affect on performance but may lead to more serious health consequences, even death (Baechle and Earle, 2000). After workouts, practices, and games, the rule of thumb is to replenish fluids at a rate of one pint for every pound of body weight loss.

Another important physical barrier in need of attention is a lack of flexibility in joints, ligaments, tendons, and muscles. By focusing on dynamic stretching, before, but especially after, practices and games, athletes will greatly reduce nagging injuries and muscle pulls, as well as improve muscle recovery and decrease delayed onset muscle soreness. Dynamic stretching entails sport-specific stretches that mimic the actions that players use during practices and games. Static stretching (i.e., slow stretch and hold for a count of 15 to 30 seconds) is still utilized and conducive to enhanced flexibility while decreasing the chance of injury. The majority of players, knowing full well the benefits of stretching, still go through the motions when they stretch.

Ensuring adequate sleep prior to practice days and games is another "little thing" that can make a difference between playing well and hoping for another chance. It is commonly accepted that each individual has a set number of sleep hours that works best for them. Knowing what this set number is and making it a priority to get the needed rest is the important next step. Another important point derived from this research is that drinking alcohol and caffeinated drinks can interfere with the sleep process. What is injected into our systems can definitely have positive and negative impacts on not only sleep but performance.

Technical/Tactical Barriers

Coaches devote most (if not all) of their time during practice sessions to technical and tactical execution. It is the aim of this book for coaches to see how they can devote more time to the mental aspects of performance while also maximizing the time given to physical and technical/tactical coaching. Applying mental-training principles during practice can maximize the quality of players' execution and improve coaching effectiveness. Most coaches would be surprised to know the many ways that they already incorporate mental-skills training into their coaching practices.

Courtesy of USC Sports Information

Figure 5-2. Players must be able to apply the technical mechanics taught in practice on the game court.

Technical and tactical coaching means the teaching of technical mechanics and reinforcing sound performance cues, in addition to the teaching of offensive and defensive schemes. Barriers exist when players do not adequately internalize these teachings (technical execution and strategic plays), and therefore are unable to apply them during "game-speed" simulations or during actual games. If players do not see how these individual drill segments fit into the "big picture" of the game, the chance of them applying the skills in pressure situations are quite low. Since "knowledge is power," sharing with players the myriad of technical mechanics involved with successful skill execution is critical. Again, these technical mechanics range from the locomotor component, to sensory, conceptual, and strategic elements.

Practicing sound mechanics in game-simulated repetitions leads to automatic skill execution, echoing the importance of simulated practice drills and improving upon the quality of practice. Players who are allowed to "go through the motions" during practice are not adequately prepared to play and will fail to fulfill their roles or offer consistent contributions to the team effort. Players must not only see how training applies to their specific roles during the game, but also how they can practice at a speed that matches game conditions. Practicing in this manner takes the synergy of the players and coaches. For example, players must apply what is done in practice onto the game court, as well as practice with game-time intensity. In addition, coaches must design practices that are game-simulated and help players to apply the training principles on the game court. Improving upon the quality of practice does require that both parties work toward the same ideals—improved game performance. Much more will be said about improving upon the quality of individual and team practice in Chapter 12.

Figure 5-3. To be able to play at the highest level, players must maximize the quality of their physical and technical training.

Chapter Summary

- Physical, technical, and mental skills are susceptible to short-term breakdowns due to the numerous variables that interfere with skill execution, which are called performance barriers.
- It is recommended that coaches determine whether the performance problem is primarily due to physical, technical, or tactical difficulties first, because these are the easiest to fix.
- Performance difficulties due to mental, team, emotional, or inspirational issues are much more complex, so coaches should rule out physical, technical, or tactical reasons first.
- Inadequate nutrition and hydration can unquestionably interfere with top performance, as much as not having the physical skills necessary to compete at the respective level.
- Applying mental training principles during practice can maximize the quality of players' execution and improve coaching effectiveness.
- Technical and tactical barriers exist when players do not adequately internalize these teachings and therefore are unable to apply them during "game-speed" simulations during practice sessions and again come game-time.

6

Barriers to Top Performance II: Team, Mental, Emotional, and Inspirational Barriers

Obstacles that can greatly impact optimal performance include team barriers (e.g., little trust within the team); mental barriers (e.g., a player's confidence level not being consistent enough); emotional barriers (e.g., resistance to change), and inspirational barriers (e.g., a lack of drive and commitment) (Figure 6-1). Chapter 5 addressed the most salient physical, technical, and tactical barriers to consistent, optimal performance.

Team Barriers

Team barriers include those variables that can interfere with players maximizing their contributions towards a collective, team effort. The term "team" will be used here to represent the entirety of all team members, but could be adapted to include positional units, such as the middles, setters, and outside hitters.

Asking the following team-related questions helps to identify potential team barrier "hotspots":

- Is the team consistent enough to make a run at the conference title each season?
- Does the team play to the level of competition (play well when facing the elite, but not so well when facing underdogs)?
- How unified is the team?

Emotional Barriers	Inspirational Barriers
• Low stress tolerance	• Disconnection between actions and beliefs
• Poor coping with time demands and frustrations	• Lack of true commitment
• Lack of social support	• Lack of honest effort
• Lack of trust in others	• Lack of purpose and passion
• Dissatisfaction, worry over uncontrollables	
• Lack of resiliency	Team Barriers
	• Unwilling to sacrifice for team
Mental Barriers	• Deciding to "go through the motions" during practices
• Poor mental recovery	• Inability to challenge teammates
• Poor/lack of coping with stress	• Does not consistently achieve preset standards
• Lack of self-confidence	• Unwilling to commit to team's goals and identity
• Irrational thinking	
• Excuse-making	• Poor communication
• Poor concentration	• Inability to hold each other accountable
• Poor problem solving skills	• Limited amount of trust
• Lack of awareness (what works and what doesn't)	• Unwilling to ask for help
• Fear of failure/mistakes	
• Fear of disappointing others	

Figure 6-1. Team, mental, and inspirational performance barriers

- Are players only partially committed to the team's pursuits?
- Do players understand and accept their roles?
- Do players blame each other when adversity hits or do they pull together and get past it?
- Do players help to lead the team through their communication and actions?
- Overall, does the team *hope* to win or *expect* to win?
- How is the team leadership? Who leads the team (other than coaches)?
- How does the team treat reserve players?
- Are teammates able to challenge each other?
- What percentage of practice sessions could be classified as quality, productive sessions?
- How much trust is there within this team?

These questions bring to light the most salient team barriers facing most volleyball teams. As Figure 6-1 shows, these barriers include a lack of commitment to team objectives, little to no sacrifice for the sake of the team effort, poor communication and

Figure 6-2. For teams to be truly cohesive, they must be able to successfully overcome team barriers.

compatibility, lack of acceptance of roles, inconsistent quality training, little team trust and leadership, and a lack of accountability. The first step in building an effective team is identifying the most salient problem areas inhibiting the process (including those that could become barriers in the future). The questions stated earlier help coaches target these specific areas for intervention. The next step is for coaches to intervene with proven strategies that will break through these team barriers, including team-building and communication interventions that are detailed in Chapter 10.

Mental Barriers

Going "beyond the X's & O's" entails an awareness of the existence of barriers and the knowledge of skill strategies to overcome them. Having your players complete the *Offensive and Defensive Mental Skill Survey* in Chapter 4 will help them gain a better awareness of the specific mental and emotional barriers currently interfering with automatic and consistent execution. Common mental barriers, as Figure 6-1 indicates, includes debilitating thoughts and self-talk, inadequate concentration and refocusing, poor confidence, inadequate preparation, fear of failure, poor coping response to stress/adversity, and unrealistic expectations. All these barriers have the potential to influence technical and mechanical execution and performance because of the interference they cause in each player's head. Do not underestimate the importance of a player trusting his own talent, skills, mental toughness, and training prior to competing. Unproductive mental activity occurs when there is a lack of trust.

To be more specific, mental interference refers to any mental activity that interferes with the automatic execution of a well-learned skill, and is also referred to as mental mechanics. This unproductive mental activity incorporates the following:

- Negative thoughts like "I hope I don't pass this ball over the net"
- Being analytical too close to execution (paralysis by overanalysis)
- Self-defeating self-talk, such as "I can't stop that outside—she hits so hard"
- Thinking about a past event, such as "the last time we played here I had a nightmare game"
- Worrying over an event in the foreseeable future, like "what if I shank this serve again?"
- Making excuses for failures, mistakes, and even successes
- Fear of making mistakes, fear of failure, fear of injury, fear of letting others down, or worrying over embarrassing oneself

How often do players think in this fashion? When they have had bad performances, how much of their thinking was like this? In most cases, when players perform well their minds are either free from this clutter or they think productively on performance-related cues or utilize confidence-building thoughts or self-talk.

Emotional Barriers

"To discuss the mental aspects of the game, we must also address the emotional and spiritual sides."
—Pete Waite, Head Volleyball Coach, Wisconsin (2002, p 304)

As Figure 6-1 indicates, the emotional barriers that can adversely affect technical execution and performance include insufficient intensity control, social disconnection, lack of resiliency to stressors, and a lack of trust in personal skills and training.

Emotional barriers such as these affect each athlete differently. Some athletes respond better in the heat of battle when they are emotionally charged up, even exhibiting anger and frustration toward their opponent, while others play better when they are more composed. Some coaches love to give the big rallying pep talks to pump up the troops, which may work for some players, but in the sport of volleyball, players need to think fast on their feet and react quickly with their hands. In general, athletes who do play better when charged up like to make their pursuit an emotionally charged, personal challenge to play to their best, beat their opponent, or both. The key is to realize what works for each athlete.

Incidents can occur if athletes do not keep a lid on their emotions, however. A good example from Major League Baseball came during game three in of the 2003 American League Playoffs. Boston Red Sox pitcher Pedro Martinez allegedly beaned a New York Yankee batter, which led to greater frustrations between the two teams. Roger Clemens then threw a brushback pitch to a Red Sox batter, which caused the benches to clear, even prompting a 72-year-old Yankee coach, Don Zimmer, to throw a punch at Martinez. Later in the game a Yankee pitcher allegedly threw a punch at a Red Sox groundskeeper. How is that for not controlling frustrations and emotions? Commentator Peter Gammons commented that this was an "embarrassing game" for the two teams and for baseball.

Examples such as this one illustrate how a lack of emotional control can affect how players bounce back after setbacks during play. Some players have low stress tolerance, so when pressure begins to pile up, mixed with additional adversity, such as mistakes or important plays, they are too frustrated to keep their minds on performance-related cues. Some players do not have coping routines to help them deal with times of stress and adversity, so as stress increases, muscle tension and/or negative thoughts increase as well, leading to more mechanical mistakes and eventually a total lapse in performance. Chapter 12 details strategies that can be used to overcome these barriers.

Inspirational Barriers

Inspiration has to do with why someone plays a particular sport and what makes him happiest while playing. Athletes play sports for hundreds of reasons—do you know why your players play volleyball? What are they getting out of the experience? Very often players' motives for playing are incongruent with their coaches' motives. Players who are not having their primary motives met are less driven to work towards their coaches' motives (e.g., better play, wins, championships), are not as satisfied with the experience, and may not try as hard or play as well.

"The key is spirit. See, the spirit is what gives you the passion on a daily basis."

—Hubie Brown, Memphis Grizzlies Coach (NBA)
(*Los Angeles Times*, 11/27/04)

Figure 6-3. Top players are driven by intrinsic factors and aspirations.

Asking players what their primary motives are for playing, as well as what their future aspirations are in volleyball will help to gain access to players' inner drives and motivations. Then, coaches can help to meet the players' primary motives, which in turn may encourage players to begin to adopt the coaches' primary motives. Coaches primarily want their teams to improve, practice hard, and get results. Players' primary motives could range from wanting to improve their games to just being affiliated with the team. Most coaches just assume that players share their motives, which in most cases is simply not true. Figure 6-1 outlines additional barriers to consider: a lack of purpose, satisfaction, and enjoyment in sporting endeavors.

Figures 5-1 and 6-1 list the most salient performance barriers. When your players or teams are hitting rough performance spells, read through these lists of performance barriers, and through process of elimination, come to the root of the problem area(s). As mentioned previously, coaches should begin with the easiest barriers to fix (physical, technical, and tactical) before proceeding to the more complex areas if needed.

Chapter Summary

• Team barriers include those variables that can interfere with players maximizing their contributions towards a collective, team effort.

Courtesy of John Voight

Figure 6-4. When athletic potential is not hindered by performance barriers, dreams do come true (twice).

- Common team barriers include a lack of commitment to team objectives, little to no sacrifice for the sake of the team effort, poor communication, lack of acceptance of roles, inconsistent quality training, and little team trust.
- Common mental barriers include debilitating thoughts and self-talk, inadequate concentration and refocusing, poor confidence, inadequate preparation, fear of failure, and poor coping responses to stress and adversity.
- Mental interference refers to any mental activity that interferes with the automatic execution of a well-learned skill, which is referred to as mental mechanics.
- Emotional barriers that can adversely affect technical execution and performance include insufficient intensity control, social disconnection, lack of resiliency to stressors, and a lack of trust in personal skills and training.
- Asking players what their primary motives are for playing, as well as what their future aspirations are in volleyball, will help you gain access to players' inner drives and current motivations.

7

Technical and Mental Mechanical Breakdowns in Execution

Previous chapters detailed the many factors that could adversely affect performance at any time. This chapter goes into greater detail regarding how these barriers interfere with the mechanical execution of passing, setting, swinging, digging, serving, and making plays.

Consistent and successful skill execution requires three interactive processes (Schmidt and Wrisberg, 2000). Performance barriers can interfere with each one of these processes, which include:

- Mental mechanics include the accurate analysis of required information—namely, specific cues picked up from what is seen and heard prior to the serve or ball contact. This is followed by the appropriate selection of movement patterns based on the motor program already established through quality reps in training and game experience.
- Mental toughness is defined as a proficiency at being able to produce productive mental states, including confidence, optimal concentration, intensity, readiness, and composed thinking and feeling during stressful times.
- Automaticity of performance includes being able to be consciously free from performance barriers. Not only do these barriers interfere with the ability to "let go" and allow talent, skill, and training to take over (trust), but they also limit performance by interfering with mechanical efficiency via breakdowns in *information processing* and *sequencing* (Moore, 1998).

Informational Processing Breakdowns

Jamming

Figure 7-1 depicts how errors in mechanical execution, namely informational processing and sequencing problems, affect performance. Fundamentally, information processing errors occur due to excessive thinking. Bill Moore (1998), a researcher and practitioner, has referred to these errors as *jamming*. When one gets "jammed," valuable information that is needed for the current play is being missed because of too much "static," or too much thinking about the wrong things. Static occurs when players overanalyze the next play ("I get so confused with the opponents' blocking"), become too apprehensive ("Will this play really work?"), or begin second-guessing ("The last time I did this play I hit it right into the block."). Static then takes up room in a player's limited attentional capacity, taking away from the important environmental cues necessary for successful execution, including defensive/offensive positioning of teammates and opponents, play calls from the setter, blocking schemes, and coaching

---

Information Processing Breakdowns

Jamming
- mechanical cause/consequence = change in technical mechanics (passing, setting, swinging, blocking)
- mental cause/consequence = excessive mental activity (static); unable to switch attention
- performance cause/consequence = overanalyze performance situations; mental errors; execution errors

Sequencing Breakdowns

Aiming
- mechanical = change in mechanics
- mental = fearful of missing the primary target, and fearful of the outcome of the play
- performance = excess tension not needed or desired

Pressing
- mechanical = change in mechanics
- mental = too outcome-oriented; unrealistic expectation of success (one out of 10 chance of getting it there)
- performance = increase in tension, which leads to a decrease in movement and technical accuracy; inaccuracy; passing-serving-hitting errors

Controlling
- mechanical = ineffective movements; change in mechanics
- mental = fearful of missing the target; fearful of outcome
- performance = inaccurate passes, serves; errors

Figure 7-1. Mechanical breakdowns: Information processing and sequencing errors

---

points from the bench and teammates. Other forms of "static" include negative thinking, thinking too much about the outcome and not on the process of execution, and inappropriate attentional focus, such as being too narrow, too broad, too external, or too internal in their focus.

Jamming can adversely affect all positional players. Players can get caught being too narrow and internal in their focus, meaning that they are only thinking about their specific assignment (limited cues) on a particular play, regardless of what could be happening around them. If they are thinking in this manner, they may miss key information that would leave them ill-prepared for the adjusted play (e.g., switches in opponent positioning, anticipation of serve location). Again, being too much "in the head" limits the amount of intuitiveness and reactionary playmaking. All players must be able to adjust at a moment's notice or they will be left in the dark—or on the bench.

Other difficulties could arise from being too broad and external in one's focus, which is discussed further in Chapter 12. Briefly, players who are too broad in focus attempt to internalize too many cues around them, some of which may be of little or no help to them. Likewise, being too external means that players are focusing on their environment too much, rather than thinking about what they need to do to get ready for the next ball.

Sequencing Breakdowns

Sequencing errors do not occur as a result of inaccurate information, but rather are due to incorrect movement execution as a result of mental interference, according to Moore (1998). Such breakdowns consist of *aiming, pressing,* and *controlling*.

Aiming

When setters or hitters are caught aiming a pass or hit, it means that they have an excessive concern for the target, such as the deep corner. Once players attempt to overly control their passes or swings, a slight change in mechanical execution usually occurs, so passes that are usually on target are either overthrown or underthrown. Servers who have an overemphasis on the specific target also get caught changing their mechanics just enough to potentially alter the flight of the ball. Although a particular serving zone is the ultimate target, some servers can get so narrow in their focus that they dismiss some important execution cues (speed, trajectory, and ball contact). Just getting the serve to the appropriate zone is not enough. The serve must have enough action and speed to make it as difficult as possible for the receiver to handle.

Pressing

Mechanics can also be altered when setters, for example, "try too hard," such as trying to force a pass to a specific spot from a difficult body position or location on the floor.

Courtesy of USC Sports Information

Figure 7-2. Setters cannot get too caught up in aiming their sets for fear of changing their mechanics.

This situation requires adding more heat to the pass or set, which adds muscle tension and changes movement sequencing. This breakdown is referred to as pressing and can also be seen with outsides or opposites who attempt a swing to a spot that has been shutdown by either a solid block or a cunning libero. Additionally, servers are guilty of pressing when they try to serve the ball too hard, thus changing their usual mechanics. Common sense would indicate that putting more force into a pass or serve would improve the play, but if this force is not the usual pace, mechanics will be changed, thereby altering the trajectory and direction of the ball. Trying to press in this fashion may cause a would-be highlight swing into a highlight miss because the automatic, reactionary swing was forced, thus changing the approach and swinging movement.

Controlling

One controlling scenario entails a hitter who is fearful of hitting into another block (or shanking another ball out-of-bounds) and thus attempts to exert too much control over the swing. This controlled swing results from excessive worry over the presumed outcome of the play and future-oriented thinking (What if I miss?), instead of just swinging the arm with a process and present-oriented style of thinking. Similarly, the mechanical execution of this controlled swing is changed somewhat, leading to what the hitter feared prior to the set—another stuff block or shank.

Servers who worry about the outcome of the upcoming serve, or who cannot seem to let go of a past missed attempt, will probably repeat the mistake due to overcontrolling the serving mechanics. Setters who are fearful of another botched set will also try to overcontrol the execution. Defensive specialists and liberos who attempt to overcontrol the pass will also change their mechanics, thus overpassing and sending the ball over the net or out of bounds.

That's why we develop muscle memory. Don't think, just do.

Figure 7-3. Successful players are able to combat mechanical breakdowns like jamming, aiming, pressing, and controlling.

What percentages of players' mistakes are due to these specific mental mechanical breakdowns? This is a very important question to discuss with players. Assisting players in acknowledging the causes of their mistakes can give them valuable information into how to correct these mechanical errors. The chapters contained in the next section, Section III, provide training strategies players can practice to effectively combat information and sequencing errors so they can not only sharpen their mental mechanics, but can also automatically execute the skills needed at game time.

Chapter Summary

- Consistent and successful skill execution requires the interactive processes of mental mechanics, mental toughness, and automaticity of performance.
- Performance barriers interfere with the ability to "let go" and allow talent, skill, and training to take over, but they also limit performance by interfering with mechanical efficiency via informational processing and sequencing breakdowns.
- When a player gets "jammed," valuable information that is needed for the current play is being missed because of too much "static."
- When hitters are caught aiming swings, it means that they have an excessive concern for a target. When they attempt to overly control their execution, there usually is a change in mechanical execution.
- Servers and hitters are sometimes guilty of pressing when they try to strike the ball too hard, thereby changing their usual mechanics.
- Players who worry about the outcome of the upcoming play, or who cannot seem to let go of a past missed play, will probably repeat the mistake(s) due to overcontrolling their mechanics.

Section III:
Training Strategies for
Automatic Execution

Good Chapter!

8

Training for Automaticity I: Combating Physical Barriers

Physical Strength and Conditioning: Physical Toughness

Volumes of resources exist that address the many aspects of physical toughness training, including: cardiovascular training, agility training, flexibility training, speed training, resistance training, plyometric training, and sport-specific conditioning (Baechle and Earl, 2000; Emma, 2003; McKown and Malone, 2003). A thorough review of these training protocols is beyond the scope of this book, but some fundamental recommendations have been posited to help coaches and athletes combat the most salient physical barrier—not being fit, fast, or strong enough to maximize performance potential. These recommendations have been encapsulated into a "Top 10" list of sport science tips, similar to one used by Matt Fitzgerald (2003).

The "Top 10" Sport Science Tips

Tip #1: Periodization of Training

The process of increasing training stress while inducing lowered frequencies/intensities of workload in time for optimal recovery and ultimately increased performance has been referred to as periodization (Baechle, Earle, & Wathen, 2000; Bompa, 1983; Loehr, 1994). In the off-season, a priority should be given to resistance training

Figure 8-1. Peaking on the court requires maximizing physical toughness.

Courtesy of AVP

(hypertrophy, strength, and power), while during the preseason the priority shifts to both sport practice and sport-specific movements. An additional priority is establishing team unity and mental toughness. The remaining chapters of this book will help with this endeavor. The highest priority of in-season training is sport practice and game execution, with attention given to the maintenance of the conditioning program, team building, and mental toughness training. Coaches should plan their seasons in this manner to maximize their players' and overall team potential. Some coaches attempt to do too much conditioning during the competitive season (the "more is better" motto), which fatigues the players when they should be recovering and getting reenergized. The references listed earlier in this section are great sources of periodization models and techniques.

Tip #2: Intensity of Training

Training intensity is considered a key variable to enhanced physical performance, whether it be striving to improve upon speed, strength, endurance, or power. Another term used to describe training intensity is training stress. More information is provided later in this chapter regarding the proper implementation of training stress, which should lead to overload and enhanced performance. It is very important for coaches to be careful in how they program intensity or stress levels to their athletes. Too little stress will result in underperforming and underachieving, while too much stress could result in training stress syndromes such as distress, staleness, or burnout. There is a science to maximizing potential, so the motto should be 'training smarter," not simply "training longer."

Tip #3: Progressive Overload Principles

The body adapts best to training regimens that gradually increase intensity/stress levels. Progressive overload applies not just to lifting greater volumes (more weight and more sets), but also longer running distances, more sprint reps, and additional sets of plyometric training exercises. Ensuring a progression in introducing greater loads and volume will not only maximize gains (in cardiovascular fitness, speed, agility, strength, and power), but also will do so in a safe manner. The "old school" approach to pre-season training should be avoided—gone are the days when players limped from drill to drill reeking of Ben Gay™ because the muscles were so sore and stiff. When players come into training already fit, their bodies will recover faster from practice to practice. Those who come into training camp unfit will struggle to keep up, and may experience fatigue and soreness, but this should not be compounded by punishment fitness sessions that will only serve to injure the player. As much as it will make coaches feel better, punishment running for unfit players is not smart training. More physical toughness aspects of pre-season training are mentioned later in this chapter.

Tip #4: Principle of Specificity

Coaches and athletes must realize that each position in volleyball requires different training modalities based upon positional needs and requirements. Also, each player differs in terms of the intensity levels that can be maintained and their rest and recovery abilities. Specificity also refers to conditioning players in game-simulated exercises and position-specific movements. Positional requirements/needs must be prioritized in the designing of strength and conditioning programs.

Tip #5: Pre-Training Evaluations

A word of caution for coaches and strength coaches on the importance of evaluating fitness and strength levels prior to specific conditioning programming: Due to specificity and progression concerns, players should be assessed prior to beginning any conditioning and fitness training programs. Having a sense of each player's baseline measures of strength, speed, power, vertical leap, and endurance is invaluable to designing specific areas of programming. Physical characteristics, age level, playing and conditioning experience, and current health status are important characteristics that need serious consideration.

Ensuring that players know appropriate lifting techniques, safety concerns, and spotting methods is critical before embarking on a program. Before plyometric training in particular, numerous assessments should be conducted. For example, players should be able to hold a half-squat position for 30 seconds before falling prior to performing plyometric exercises (Potachu & Chu, 2000). Other pre-assessment standards have been established for speed workouts as well (Baechle, Earle, & Wathen, 2000).

Tip #6: Fueling the Machine

Detailed information on eating for enhanced functioning and optimal performance is provided throughout this chapter. Specific areas addressed include information on critical nutrients, effects of hydration, content of pre-event meals, and eating for optimal recovery.

Tip #7: Recovery Training

Athletes and coaches at the top levels of sport have recently considered "recovery" as an important aspect of training. Recovery stands for more than just resting outside of training. Recovery could include treatments, such as taking ice baths or whirlpools to help heal sore muscles, or doing extra stretching and flexibility work after hard training sessions. Recovery could be passive, like watching video, using imagery, or engaging in a favorite hobby. Recovery could also be active, like cross-training, yoga, or periods of lower-intensity workouts. Recovery training is not only important for physiological reasons, such as taxing other energy systems and muscle groups, but also for mental and emotional recovery. Taking time outside of the sport can really help to revitalize and restore energy and motivation.

Tip #8: Hydration

Since athletes usually replace only two-thirds of water that they lose through sweat, they put themselves at risk of dehydration and decreased performance. More information is provided about the importance of proper hydration later in this chapter.

Tip #9: Dynamic Flexibility

Static stretching, whereby a stretch is held for 30 to 40 seconds, has been the most recommended form of active flexibility training for years, but dynamic stretching is gaining popularity. In dynamic stretching, sport-specific movements are used that mimic the speed of specific movements used during play. For example, hitters and blockers who stretch with a stretch band can simulate the hitting action while fully preparing the muscles, tendons, and ligaments. A third type of stretching, proprioceptive neuromuscular facilitation (PNF), may be the best form of stretching due to the three types of muscle actions utilized to elicit the stretch—namely, the hold-relax-contract cycles. PNF, which is a form of partner stretching, has long been used to incorporate both passive and active stretching.

Tip #10: Quality Training and Conditioning

Chapter 13 describes in detail a model for improving upon the quality of practice, which can be applied directly to volleyball training and strength and conditioning training. This model is based upon viewing training sessions as dynamic processes that include responsibilities from both athletes and coaches. The four main aspects to the model include improving upon coach and athlete attitude towards training, preparation practices, execution strategies, and quality control methods post-practice.

Off-Season Conditioning

For coaches to be able to effectively apply these "Top 10" tips to their teams, players must come into pre-season with some semblance of physical conditioning. Coaches continually stress the importance of off-season conditioning. These same coaches provide off-season conditioning programs, which normally incorporate the following components: weight training, cardiovascular training, speed work, agility, plyometrics, and flexibility. Although the major objective of off-season conditioning is to prepare the body for the grueling stress of pre-season/training camp, there are other prime benefits to an organized conditioning program. In addition to increasing physical toughness, forcing a player to work through and beyond their "comfort levels" on his own over the summer months will greatly elevate his mental and emotional toughness. Physical, mental, and emotional toughening involve increasing one's capacity to endure stress. A leader in the field of toughness training defines "toughness" as "the ability to consistently perform toward the upper range of your talent and skill regardless of competitive circumstances" (Loehr, 1994, p. 18).

If players give maximal effort during the off-season during their physical conditioning and play, they will experience increased gains in their physical, mental, and emotional toughness. Yet if a less-than-maximal effort is given during their off-season preparation and conditioning, numerous consequences will occur. Figure 8-2 details the many consequences that occur when athletes undertrain, or decide not to put in the effort and time necessary (Voight, 2000a). These consequences not only adversely affect the individual, but the team as well. Consequences of coming into training camp undertrained could include negative effects on one's physiology, mental and emotional functioning, and skill training and performance.

The physical, mental, and emotional benefits of putting in maximal effort and time on the off-season conditioning/playing program are countless. Players who "cheat" their off-season conditioning can always be detected, especially if coaches recognize the numerous symptoms mentioned in Figure 8-2, many of which will affect players' thinking, emotions, and physiology, not to mention the team-wide consequences that may surface as training camp progresses. Recognizing those who did not come into training camp ready is only the first step, with the next being how to deal with this inefficient preparation.

In general, coaches strategically design each training camp session down to the last minute and the last play. When one or more players come into training camp ill prepared, most coaches must make changes, often drastic changes, to these strategic plans. Instead of focusing primarily on certain technical or tactical aspects, coaches must spend more time than originally planned on fitness-related activities. Instead of

Physical Consequences	Mental Consequences
• major/minor pain	• poor concentration
• muscle soreness	• poor problem solving
• illness	• chronic mental fatigue
• decreased workrate	• mental mistakes
• lack of effort	• negative thinking
• incidence or continuance of injury	• decrease in confidence
• sleeping/eating problems	Emotional Consequences
• decrease in performance	• low motivation
Skill Consequences	• moodiness
• lack of quality	• anxiety
• less than full-speed	• nervousness
• rigid, clumsy performance	• lack of enjoyment
• going through the motions	• anger
• poor execution habits	• sadness

Figure 8-2. Consequences of undertraining

being "ahead of the game" at the beginning of training camp, a team will begin the season behind the rest of the pack. Once this happens, it is important for coaches to avoid pushing their players too much and instead attempt to get their players caught up on their fitness. Poor fitness levels can lead to injury and other consequences, including training stress syndromes, which are discussed later in this chapter. It is very important to continue to stress to your players the importance of "toughening up" in the off-season, or players will continually show up undertrained, thereby kick-starting the debilitating consequences not only to them, but also to their teammates, training camp, and potentially the success of the team throughout the season.

Implementation of Training Stress

A final point about physical toughness is for coaches to be aware of the careful implementation of training stress. How many coaches know exactly how much to practice and how much to "push" their players physically and technically? To optimize peak performance, athletes, coaches, and strength coaches often adopt and reinforce accelerated training regimens. These usually take the form of large increments of training stress, longer training and conditioning sessions, and shorter recovery periods, all of which could prove detrimental to the individual's physical, psychological, and emotional standing.

The ESPN made-for-television movie, "The Junction Boys," showed Paul "Bear" Bryant's coaching methods during his first season at Texas A&M. The grueling practices during the hottest time of the day with little to no water were standard throughout his training camp. As it turned out, after waves of players left training camp in the wee hours of the morning, by the time the season came around his remaining players were so depleted and worn out that they finished the season with only two wins. Although this depicted an earlier era, the message taken from this movie—along with the many other stories about legendary coaching practices—is that knowing the difference between toughening players and breaking them down is critical for the well-being and performances of players. With the help of sport science researchers, numerous training stress syndromes have been documented that can accompany inadequate training practices that range from overtraining, underrecovery, distress, staleness, and burnout.

For athletes to get fitter, stronger, and tougher mentally and emotionally, stress is required. According to Loehr (1994), for athletes to perform to their potential they have to increase their ability to handle three kinds of stress—physical, emotional, and mental—and become stronger, more responsive, and resilient to these stresses. Most sport and strength coaches at the elite levels realize that training stress needs to be carefully manipulated for optimal performance to occur. Careful adjustment of the level, intensity, and frequency of training stress to a point where the demands placed upon a particular system of the body are greater than it is used to handling involves a training principle commonly referred to as overload. After numerous bouts of overload, adaptation, and partial recovery, which could last for days or weeks depending upon the sport and competitive schedule, a period of reduced training overload is induced, referred to as tapering. Tapering normally occurs days or weeks prior to important competitions and allows the athletes' bodies to recover, compensate, and adapt to the periods of heavy training. Such a program adequately prepares athletes for maximal performances come game day. Negative adaptations occur when athletes are unable to adapt to overloading practice regimens or competitive stressors.

Training Stress Syndromes

Negative adaptation occurs when any of the competitive stressors are heightened beyond an optimal point and continue over a period of time. The training stress syndrome is initiated by overtraining and underrecovery, and because of this excessive training stress without adequate rest, fatigue results, followed by the more debilitating syndromes of distress, staleness, and burnout.

Overtraining and Underrecovery

Overtraining has been defined by Smith (1999) as an excessive overload of training stress without adequate rest or recovery from this stress, which results in excessive fatigue, performance decrements, psychological/emotional disturbances, and an inability to train. An athlete who experiences these stages has coping systems that are progressively getting taxed, leading to the possibility of the athlete's adaptive mechanisms—both mental and physical—to be jeopardized. Athletes who continue to experience excessive training stress can regress from this overtrained stage into a distressed condition.

Distress and Staleness

It is believed that distress is an acute response to being overtrained and therefore can be treated by short-term interventions. If appropriate short-term interventions are not implemented at this distress stage, and if overtraining continues, athletes can regress further into the staleness syndrome, which is a serious manifestation of overtraining. Staleness is associated with numerous negative effects, especially behavioral, mental, emotional, and technical symptoms, as shown in Figure 8-3 (Voight, 2003). Distress and staleness are primarily caused by the physical and mental demands of increased training. Once stale, athletes who are exposed to greater increments of physical, mental, and emotional stress can begin exhibiting symptoms of burnout that represent a more severe reaction to overtraining.

Technical Execution	*Mentality*
• monotonous practice sessions	• mental fatigue
• lack of quality execution	• lack of focus
• loss of coordination	• lack of motivation
• poor communication with coaches	• confused thinking
• confusion over role	• poor problem solving
Workrate	• negative thinking
• decreased workrate	• depression
• going through the motions in prac-tices/games	*Emotionality*
• affected by pain, soreness, and injury	• irritability
• decreased power output	• moodiness
Physiology	• boredom
• weight loss	• sadness
• higher resting heart rate (HR)	• anxiety
• impeded respiration	• lack of enjoyment
• delayed return to normal HR	• negativism
• increased muscle fatigue	• loss of self-esteem
	• social withdrawal

Figure 8-3. Consequences of staleness due to overtraining/underrecovery

Burnout

The major discriminating variable between staleness and burnout is that cognitive (mental) factors, such as a loss of interest and motivation, are reported to directly relate to burnout. Another distinguishing variable from the other phases of the training syndrome is that once athletes experience burnout, voluntary or involuntary withdrawal from sport can be inevitable (Silva, 1990). Generally, burnout is characterized by physical, mental, and emotional withdrawal from activities that once were sources of great satisfaction and enjoyment but have been replaced by physical and psychological stress.

Successfully defeating the effects of distress and staleness in athletes can be accomplished via a multistage process. Intervention begins with gaining a better understanding of the causes of these training stress syndromes, over and above training volume, and the emotional, physical, and psychological stress experienced. Numerous other factors have been found by Henschen (1986) to contribute to the debilitating effects of distress and staleness, including length of the competitive season, training monotony, lack of positive reinforcement, abusiveness by coaches, stringent rules, high levels of competitive stress, perceived low accomplishment, and boredom.

Armed with these two important pieces of information (understanding the causes and recognizing the symptomology), appropriate intervention strategies can then be used to eliminate the debilitating effects of these syndromes, as well as optimize athletes' methods of coping. Preventing fatigue and underrecovery, distress, and staleness takes great care and oversight from the entire coaching staff. Coaches who are more aware of the training stress syndromes and are diligent about monitoring their athletes' physiological, emotional, psychological, and performance functioning, are in better positions to eliminate or prevent the regressive continuance of the training stress syndrome. The intervention strategies can be categorized into three major areas: physical, mental, and performance-related interventions. These interventions, which are shown in Figure 8-4, are targeted for both players and coaches, as both are affected by the consequences of the training stress syndromes.

Physical	Mental
• physical rest and recovery	• recovering mentally and emotionally
• energizing food	• setting short-term goals for practice
• periodization principles (tapering)	• self-challenges
• variety of training methods/exercises	• one-drill-at-a-time mentality
• incentives and rewards	• process-focused; improve on last
• competitions within training sessions	performance
• showers and massages	• energized thinking and self-talk
	• use of pre-practice routines

Performance	
• organized, competitive training sessions	• incorporating new drills
• reducing the monotony of practice (variety)	• asking for player input (favorite drills)

Figure 8-4. Training stress syndrome interventions

The final aspect of effective interventions for eliminating staleness is continual feedback, reinforcement, and evaluation. Being aware of the potential causes, the signs and symptoms, and the primary goals of interventions represents a "three-pronged attack" on the deleterious effects of training stress syndromes. Intervention success can be subjectively and objectively evaluated once clear goals are made. Murphy (1996) identified numerous questions that can be used to evaluate the effectiveness of staleness interventions in reaching specific goals:

- Are athletes performing better?
- Do the athletes feel better about their lives, performances, and fitness?
- How is their communication with teammates and coaches?
- Do athletes feel psychologically and emotionally stronger?
- Are athletes healthier and less injury prone?
- Are athletes staying connected with their teammates?
- Do athletes feel adequately rested, recovered, and energized from practice session to practice session?
- Do athletes have adequate coping resources to deal with training stress?

Continually asking athletes these questions and obtaining their feedback regarding the physical, emotional, and psychological adjustments they have made to increased training stress is critical if coaches want to minimize training stress syndromes. Since increases in training stress, volume, and intensity will continue to be implemented by coaches and athletes who aspire for greatness, helping players cope and adapt to these high training loads should be a primary concern for all involved, including athletes, coaches, strength coaches, sport psychologists, parents, and administrators. Educating all parties about training principles, causes and symptoms of training stress syndromes, and interventions designed to reduce or eliminate the effects of these syndromes will go a long way toward minimizing the number of athletes who unnecessarily suffer from distress, staleness, and burnout.

Nutrition—Eating to Win

Most coaches appreciate the importance of eating nutritional foods prior to training and playing. But how many know what types of foods produce the most energy? How about the timing of eating prior to games? Not eating or hydrating properly can be a large performance barrier for any player. This section outlines the research-based recommendations regarding fueling up the "machine."

For peak athletic performance, the two primary dietary goals for most elite athletes are eating to maximize performance and eating for optimal body composition, according to Reimers and Ruud (2000). According to the National Strength and Conditioning Association (NSCA), the best diets for performance enhancement are those that are individualized. What works for one athlete may not work for another. Individualized diets for volleyball players should adhere to accepted guidelines. All athletes should:

Figure 8-5. Training volume must be properly controlled for players to perform to the utmost of their capacities.

Courtesy of USC Sports Information

- Monitor appropriate calorie intake. For example, general caloric intake guidelines for athletes ages 17 to 23: 5'7" and 5'8" = 2900 calories per day; 5'9" = 3100; 5'10" = 3200; 5'11" = 3300; 6' = 3400; 6'1" = 3500, and so on (USC, 2003).
- Consume appropriate nutrient levels to prevent deficiencies.
- Follow diets containing recommended servings per food group.
- Avoid omitting food groups, since this can lead to deficiencies in specific nutrients.
- Consume significant amounts of the macronutrients, namely proteins (20% of calories), carbohydrates (60% of calories), and lipids (less than 30%).
- Avoid no-fat or low-fat diets because these diets lead to deficiencies in key nutrients.
- Consume adequate amounts of vitamins and minerals in the diet.

- Gain weight safely (1 to 2 pounds a week) by eating 350 to 750 calories above daily requirements, and eating five high-calorie meals each day.
- Lose weight safely (1 to 2 pounds a week) by eating no less than 2000 calories a day (could be more), and eating nutritionally balanced, varied meals five times a day.
- Use pre-game meals to properly hydrate and energize for peak performance.

The reference section at the back of the book includes websites to visit for more information on sound nutritional practices.

The pre-event meal can do more to hinder than to enhance performance. The purpose of the pre-game meal is to maximize glycogen stores, or energy, minimize digestion during competition, provide fluids, and avoid gastric distress. Numerous factors must be taken into consideration when planning this meal, such as general dietary patterns and foods normally eaten by players (the pre-game meal is not the time to introduce players to exotic foods), timing of the meal, specific components to the meal, and specific foods to be included. Include fluids in the meal, especially water and sport drinks, and nothing caffeinated, as caffeine is a diuretic and takes water out of the body.

The pre-game meal should be eaten three and a half to four hours prior to competition. This should be time enough to allow the stomach to be relatively empty. In addition, the meal should consist mainly of complex carbohydrates, such as pastas, grains, vegetables, rice, and beans. Muscle carbohydrate (glycogen) depletion impairs performance. Carbohydrate-rich foods replenish this much-needed muscle carbohydrate. Simply put, carbohydrates are converted into blood sugar (glucose), which muscles burn for energy; any unused glucose gets stored in muscles and the liver as glycogen for future energy. Glycogen is the preferred fuel because it is easier to burn than fat, and is more readily available to the muscles. When the muscle glycogen gets depleted, blood glucose is required, and it is very difficult to maintain energy levels during extended play with glucose as the energy source (Roberts, 2001).

The meal should also include protein. While protein content should be somewhat limited because it takes longer to digest and absorb than carbohydrates, protein intake will assist in avoiding sensations of hunger. Some examples of proteins include tuna, peanut butter, eggs, fish, chicken, and red meat. Also, limit the intake of fat, such as mayonnaise, butter, oil, salad dressing, sour cream, gravy, and margarine, because of the prolonged process of digestion, which could last up to eight hours. The problem with prolonged digestion during play is that some blood and energy stores that could be used by the exercising muscles will be redistributed to the stomach to aid in digestion.

Certain foods should be avoided, including foods with spicy ingredients that could cause heartburn and indigestion, and milk products because they can cause gastric distress in some players. Greasy foods should also be avoided because of the excess fat and the slower rates of digestion and emptying.

Hydration—Drinking to Win

Research has indicated water losses, through sweating, of 1 or 2% of body weight can impair mental and physical functioning, according to Chichester (2002). When water is not replaced, total blood volume and oxygen delivery via the blood is impaired. The earliest symptoms of dehydration include loss of concentration and increased fatigue, since the brain and heart need water to maintain electrolyte balance and proper functioning. The more dehydrated athletes get, the more performance suffers. It has been reported by *Hydrate* (2002) that a 3 to 5% drop in fluid level causes a 10% drop in contractile strength, an 8% drop in speed, and can cause headaches, dizziness, cramping, and nausea.

Tell your players not to rely on thirst as an accurate indicator of the need for water. Those who wait until this point can only put back between 50 to 75% of the body's need for fluids. In addition, knowing each player's weight pre- and post-workout can be a useful method of keeping track of weight loss. For each pound of weight lost, the player has lost one pint of fluid, and thus, needs to replace one pint of fluid. Over the course of a week, if players are losing five to 10 pounds, this indicates substantial fluid loss, since fat loss does not occur this quickly (Reimers & Ruud, 2000).

Each player should drink at least two cupfuls of water two hours before training or game play—this allows the kidneys 60 to 90 minutes to process excess fluids—and drink an additional one to two cups 15 minutes prior, which lowers the body's core temperature and replaces sweat loss. Additionally, sipping more water every 15 to 20 minutes during a game or practice should keep players properly hydrated. The more strenuous the training, the hotter the temperature, and the larger the athlete, the greater fluid intake should be before, during, and after training/game play. Fluid loss also indicates a loss in electrolytes and sodium, both of which help regulate water distribution. Sport drinks are quite useful in replacing sodium, as well as critical electrolytes including potassium, chloride, and magnesium.

Although some research has indicated that using urine color to monitor hydration levels is an inaccurate method, not all researchers agree. The old adage is to strive for a pale color after training or play. Players should be instructed to drink several cups of water and sport drinks post-game. Water is an ideal fluid replacement, though flavored sports drinks may promote greater drinking frequency, and these drinks may be more effective than water in rehydration, as they contain electrolytes, sugar, and carbohydrates. This is especially true after significant weight loss has occurred through sweating (Reimers & Ruud, 2000).

Recovery—Eating and Drinking to Replenish

Research has shown that consuming carbohydrates and protein within 30 to 60 minutes after playing helps to reload muscles in 12 to 16 hours. If this "window" of opportunity is not taken advantage of, players may have less energy, which may affect motivation and drive the next day. The ratio of carbohydrates to proteins has been recommended to be three to one. For recovery purposes, carbohydrates restore muscle glycogen, and protein helps to repair and rebuild muscles and assists in transporting carbohydrates to the muscles (Liddane, 2002). Ed Burke, an expert in recovery and creator of the Endurox R-4 sports drink, recommends that players eat a high-carbohydrate, high-protein "snack" within the recovery "window." He also recommends that a meal be eaten two to four hours post-game with the following nutritional make-up: carbohydrate (65%), fat (20%), and protein (15%) (Roberts, 2001).

Courtesy of USC Sports Information

Figure 8-6. Making recovery training an active part of the practice routine helps players replenish their energy for game-time

Chapter Summary

- It is very important for coaches to be careful in how they program intensity or stress levels to their players. Too little stress will result in underperforming and underachieving, while too much stress could result in training stress syndromes such as distress, staleness, or burnout.

- Consequences of coming into training camp undertrained could include negative effects on physiology, mental and emotional functioning, and skill training and performance.

- Distress and staleness are primarily caused by the physical and mental demands of increased training. Once stale, players who are exposed to greater increments of stress can begin exhibiting symptoms of burnout.

- For peak athletic performance, two primary dietary goals for most elite athletes are eating to maximize performance and eating for optimal body composition.

- Research has shown that consuming carbohydrates and protein within 30 to 60 minutes after playing helps to reload muscles in 12 to 16 hours.

9

Training for Automaticity II: Combating Technical-Tactical Barriers

Technical/Tactical Proficiency

Improving upon players' technical mechanics, as well as improving the transfer of tactical lessons learned in practice onto the game court, takes deliberate effort on the part of both athletes and coaches. Because of the importance to optimal performance, improving upon deliberate practice is discussed in full in Chapter 13, where a model is presented for improving upon the quality of practice via enhancing player and coach attitude, preparation, execution, and monitoring processes. Each component of the model includes numerous strategies coaches and players can incorporate to improve technical and tactical execution.

Some athletes sabotage their technical and tactical execution prior to playing via mental misses. Mental misses can happen to any player, especially setters, hitters, defensive specialists, blockers, and servers.

Consistent players usually have high levels of confidence and truly believe that on any given play something good will happen. Consistent performers are usually very proficient at blocking out distractions and focusing on each play, while also practicing their craft relentlessly. On the other hand, those positional players who are "streaky" and inconsistent may not be physically and mentally committed to improving their total games. This lack of overall commitment can take many forms, including the belief that practicing fundamental techniques is a waste of time, that plays will be made in critical situations without practicing, and that it is acceptable to go through the motions in practice instead of performing quality, focused reps. Essentially, these players do not realize the importance of the mental side of passing, blocking, swinging, and serving.

Inconsistent players could be missing key plays before the ball is even played to them because they make too many mental mistakes prior to the play. Mental mistakes primarily occur across five mental skill attributes:

- Confidence in one's abilities
- Trust in preparation and skills
- Focus on the important components of the skill, like specific cues
- Commitment to improving skill execution in practice
- Executing one play at a time

Players who are fortunate enough to have these mental traits execute their skills in a smooth, effortless, automatic fashion. Players who "mentally miss" their chances normally lack one or more of these mental traits, or are unable to get back to their usual game when they are "off" and playing poorly. The seven typical mental mistakes are listed in the following section, along with ways to correct these mental mistakes. Most of the examples listed are primarily for setters and hitters, yet these mental misses can easily be applied to all positions.

Typical Mental Misses

The "Hit and Hope" Player

Once the ball leaves the fingertips "hit and hope" players pray that it gets to its primary target. This type of player lacks confidence in his ability to connect certain passes or make the right pass or the right blocking read. He lacks trust in his preparation, possibly because he has not prepared adequately enough through focused practice. He hopes that luck will accompany these passes, swings, serves, or blocks, and almost relies on the "volleyball gods" to deliver. Changing such a player into a consistent "playmaker" takes old-fashioned hard work and focused repetition, and the realization that only he can change his practice habits and improve his confidence. Missed hits, bad passes, and miscues are often the result of this type of thinking.

The "Do or Die" Player

A player whose sole focus is on outcome, like being the game MVP or simply on winning the game or match, can often distract himself enough to miss the play before it is happens. When a couple of points do not go as planned, due to bad passes or missed blocks, he is devastated. Although most of the pressure players perceive is self-imposed, a few situations (e.g., serving for game point) exist when actual pressure is present. A "do or die" player realizes this pressure and heaps even more on himself by saying, "I need to make this set to keep the score close, to win the game,...", or "If I miss another set my hitters will get frustrated." This increased pressure due to outcome creates more stress that can get translated into excess muscle tension or defeatist thinking, which are not advantageous to any player who is in need of fluid, relaxed execution. See the section that follows on the "flexed" player for more details on this aspect of pressure. Do or die players need to learn how to focus more on the process of executing the skill and less on the outcome by using technical cues, which consist of one to two aspects of the needed skill. Setters may want to focus on a "quick release," a "smooth touch," or some other cue that helps the process of completing sets, rather than focusing only on how important a particular set may be.

Courtesy of SCVC & Ralf's Photography

Figure 9-1. It is important for coaches to help players become more aware of "mental misses."

The "Fader" Player

A player who tends to "fade" in critical times is easily distracted by either internal or external forces, or both. His focus fades from *external* distractions, such as the importance of the situation, crowd noise, or visual distractions, to *internal* distractions, like how he is dealing with the pressure of the moment, the importance of the play, or how he played the last time against this opponent. Since attentional capacity is limited, a player who attends to too many cues, especially irrelevant cues, sets himself up for mental misses, which have technical consequences such as poorly timed hitting or blocking approaches, errant passes, and scattered sets—all due to "being too much in the head." This is called "jamming" and is discussed in Chapter 7. Jamming occurs when athletes fail to focus only on the most pertinent cues and information necessary for successful execution. A player who fades needs to work on being aware of what he is focusing on prior to, and during, play execution. Once he becomes aware of where his focus lies, the next step is to focus only on the most relevant cues. Coaches can be a big help in assisting players in this process. Once players consistently focus on specific cues, the distractions will be blocked out, resulting in an automated, free-flowing performance.

The "Flexed" Player

A player who is "flexed" is tight and tense due to his fear of missing sets, hits, blocks, or serves. Fear of failure can lead to excessive tension in the shoulders, biceps, triceps, and forearms, thereby causing a normally smooth action to turn into a rigid, stiff motion. Hitters have stated how tight their shoulder muscles can get in times of stress and pressure. This change in technical form, often called "pressing," can be reversed by learning how to relax these critical muscle groups via muscle relaxation exercises, relaxation breathing, and pre-hit routines that can enhance mental and physical readiness. A player who is aware of "pressing" is well on his way to changing his performance woes.

The "Hot/Cold" Player

A "hot and cold" player is simply streaky. When "hot handed" he will complete his sets and make plays. But if any part of his game is off, he carries this with him to the next serve, resulting in "cold" spells. Truly competitive players are able to remain consistent in their play by being consistent "thinkers"—they do not allow swings in game momentum or periods of good/poor play cause them to change their approach, confidence, and readiness. A consistently high level of playing confidence can be ensured through pre-serve routines, coping routines used to help refocus after mistakes or great plays by opponents, positive imagery, and self-coaching affirmations. These techniques are discussed in detail in Chapter 12.

The "Mechanical" Player

A mechanical player allows his left brain to dominate his processing by focusing too much of his attention on the specific mechanics of the necessary technique. These technical motions should be so habitual and well learned that thinking about particular elements right before execution becomes a major distraction. Sound mental mechanics mean being able to maintain a focus prior to execution on productive elements, thus freeing the mind of distraction. This results in automatic execution—a point worth repeating. For example, a mechanical setter may change a portion of his pre-set routine and setting action due to a lack of confidence and trust in his mechanics just prior to execution. This could be one of the reasons why he is constantly thinking and tinkering with his setting. Establishing a consistent pre-set routine and setting action is critical for mechanical players. Keep in mind that focusing on one to two general technical cues is recommended, such as "smooth" or "quick delivery" for passers/setters. These general cues are linked to specific actions, which helps to ensure efficient mechanics. "Smooth," for example, is recited prior to the set because the setter has programmed this word to trigger a relaxed, smooth, automatic arm-hand-finger action. The use of multiple technical cues is not recommended because this will internally distract the "mechanical" player and cause him to think too much prior to delivery. Middles, opposites, and defensive specialists can all incorporate general cues, helping them to free their minds and automatically execute once called upon.

The "Counter" Player

A player who gets caught up counting his hitting errors, serving errors, blocking errors, and playing time—especially from game to game—is only bringing (or keeping) himself down via lowered confidence and heightened anxiety. Meanwhile, he is heightening the pressure for successful future outcomes. Players who know exactly how many mistakes they have made are too outcome-focused and are guilty of being "counters." To break the cycle of counting these miscues, players must become process-focused rather than outcome-focused by taking one play at a time and utilizing a consistent pre-serve routine that includes the use of one to two general passing cues. Counting mistakes will only lead to more missed plays.

Chapter Summary

- Inconsistent players could be missing key plays before the ball is even served because they make too many mental mistakes prior to the play.
- Mental mistakes occur across five mental-skill attributes: confidence, trust, focus, commitment, and executing one play at a time.
- Mental mistakes encompass not being confident enough ("hit and hope" players), and being too outcome-focused ("do or die" players), too easily distracted ("fader" players), too tight and tense ("flexed" players), too streaky ("hot/cold" players), too analytical ("mechanical" players), and counting mistakes ("counter" players).
- Players who mentally miss their chances can combat their barriers by enhancing their mental toughness skills.

10

Training for Automaticity III:
Combating Team Barriers

Effective teamwork can often be the difference between success and failure. This can be exemplified by the paradox in which teams full of talented players fail to use their individual resources and fall short of expectations, while teams with less talent and resources prevail (Hardy and Crace, 1997). Effective teamwork has been defined as (Carron, Spink, & Prapavessis, 1997; Yukelson, 1997):

- Taking advantage of the various abilities and backgrounds of team members
- Interacting and working toward shared goals
- Balancing the needs of the team with the needs of the individual members
- Structuring methods of communication

Chapter 6 covers the many barriers that can sabotage a team's pursuit of greatness, including an unwillingness to sacrifice for the team, poor communication, lack of quality practice, inability to hold teammates accountable, unwillingness to help teammates, and a lack of trust. Lencioni (2002) identified additional team barriers, titled the "five dysfunctions" of a team, which include absence of trust, fear of conflict, lack of commitment, avoidance of accountability, and inattention to results.

According to Lencioni, an absence of trust means that team members are not open with each other about their thoughts and feelings. Once this occurs, team members are not honest about their feedback for fear of conflict and having to share real ideas in an open discussion. Due to an inability to openly share ideas, team members do not commit to team decision and objectives. Since team members do not share common ideals, there is an avoidance of accountability, which then leads to an overindulgence of individual agendas rather than a collective effort toward team objectives.

Successfully defeating these barriers will create teams that trust one another enough to have open discussions, which will lead to a greater commitment to team ideals. This will allow team members to hold each other accountable to these standards, thereby leading to a collective effort toward achieving team goals. Team trust is a fragile concept—if one element is lacking, there will be fallout. This chapter emphasizes several examples coaches and teams can utilize to steer clear from these barriers and prosper.

To assist athletes, coaches, and teams enhance upon these critical components of effective teamwork while also steering clear of the team barriers, a team intervention called team building can be utilized to positively affect team processes and team performance. The aim of these team-building strategies is to get all team members "on the same page" in terms of the team's direction and primary objectives, as well as forge an agreement on the team standards and everyone's particular roles and responsibilities. A carefully designed team-building program is a proactive way to combat potential team barriers before they occur. Although using a program does not guarantee total team harmony, it gives coaches and players a forum where they can discuss goals, team rules, and standards, and address potential problem areas before they develop. The framework behind this sample team-building program consists of the following components. Each of these specific areas is then discussed in greater detail.

- Team motives and preferences for team progress
- An accepted team identity—what the team will be known for by others
- A shared vision via setting short-term process goals that lead to accomplishing long-term outcome goals
- Individual and team accountability to preset standards and goals
- Collaborative communication, teamwork, and trust
- Team-bonding activities in the off-season, pre-season, and during the season

Individual/Team Motives

One way to maximize a player's motivation is to match his preferences and motives with your own motives and behaviors. For example, a player whose primary motive is to improve upon his game enough to earn a scholarship at a top school is going to want demanding technical sessions and would prefer a coach who will encourage him to accomplish this goal. If the player's preferences and motives are matched, he will be more satisfied and motivated to pursue his goals. If the players' preferences and motives are not matched by the coach, dissatisfaction and underachievement may result. This dynamic also applies to team motives and preferences.

"When the team's goals are consistent with a player's professional goals, that player is a lot more likely to be a team player."
— Pat Williams, Senior Executive VP, Orlando Magic (1997, p. 129)

The dynamics of a team could be such that, although players may "talk a big game" about improving enough to compete for championships, the (underlying) primary motives could be more socially-related, for example. Players may enjoy being members of an elite team and enjoy being around their teammates. Until these motives and preferences are met by the coaches' motives, which may include wanting to win the league championship, goals will not be adequately pursued. Gaining a better understanding of players' motives and preferences can aid in not only maximizing motivation but also in getting everyone "on the same page," regarding the goals for the team.

Obtaining this information is as easy as asking each player what his primary motives are for playing, and what teammate and coach behaviors he prefers. To get a better idea of what specific preferences your players have in terms of the feedback provided them by coaches and teammates, ask them to do the following:

- List three things you would like to see the coaches do and say this pre-season/season that would help:
  ✓ this team accomplish its goals
  ✓ you accomplish your goals

- List three things you would like to see your teammates do and say this pre-season/season that would help:
  ✓ this team accomplish its goals
  ✓ you accomplish your goals

This information will give coaches a better idea of what "buttons" to push with each of the players. It certainly does not mean that you have to always abide by these preferences, but it does help provide a guideline. For example, if a player would like to see his coach "get on me when I lose focus or when I begin to go through the motions," this gives coaches some valuable information in terms of the best method by which to get this player back into the game mentally.

Team Identity

Getting an idea of how the team would like to be perceived by others, such as opponents, fans, or family members, is another way of getting the most from your players. Asking the team to clarify their "team identity" can elicit player feedback regarding goals, motives, and how they would like to be seen and known by others. Armed with this information, you can hold your team accountable to this ideal team image.

Ask each member the following questions:
- How would you want opponents to view the team?
- How would you like to be perceived during practices; what would spectators of the practices say about the team?
- How would you want your team to be perceived by game officials or the media?

Use this information to help develop your team identity. Once established, any time you see players who are not showing their chosen identity, remind them about it. Also emphasize when you do see them demonstrating the ideal they have created. More is said about these "coachable moments" in a later section.

> *"This game ... can give you a lot of things, but it can't give you a championship. You've got to earn that. And unless you're willing to pay the collective price—to play as a team—you will not get it."*
> —Bill Parcells, Head Coach, Dallas Cowboys (Williams, 1997, p. 115)

Team and Individual Goals

Goal-setting is effective in influencing performance by enhancing motivation, self-confidence, commitment, effort, and mental readiness. Research has shown that pursuing goals conveys information to the players about their capabilities and progress, thus enhancing confidence and motivation to continue striving toward excellence. A common analogy states that setting effective goals is similar to using a road map before embarking on a long trip. Mapping the way before a trip is obviously important for arriving at the destination safely and efficiently. Applying this thinking to a team's journey to the predetermined destination, whether that be a conference, state, or national championship is highly recommended.

To kick-start this goal-setting process, present the following questions to your players:
- What would you like to be doing with volleyball in five years?

- What do you want to accomplish in volleyball this year?
- What does this team want to accomplish this year?
- What are some areas of your game that you need to improve?
- What are some areas that the team needs to improve?

Having players answer these questions, especially during the off-season or pre-season practice, will get them thinking about their own games as well as the team game, and what aspects of both must be improved upon. Players' and coaches' responses to these questions can then be shared and used to devise short- and long-term goals. Individual and team goals can be quite empowering if used properly through shared input and continual evaluation and follow-up.

SMART goals are recommended to develop a goal-setting program for your players and team.

S = Specific: These are not "do your best" goals, but instead specific aspects needing improvement (also called action goals).

M = Measurable: You should be able to evaluate whether a goal was achieved via the use of numbers or objective measures.

A = Achievable: A goal should be within a player's or team's capabilities.

R = Realistic: All goals should be challenging ones that are not too easy or too difficult.

T = Time-based: You should be able to assign a set target date when a goal will be achieved.

Each of the various types of goals has its proper place in the goal-setting process. Though many players may find *outcome* goals motivating, they should be used minimally, since outcomes may be beyond a player's immediate control. Examples of outcome goals include winning games, championships, and awards.

Process goals should be used as stepping stones (short-term goals) that lead players to accomplish their long range goals. These short-term process goals should be specific technical, tactical, mental, and/or physical aspects that players are driven to accomplish. When players attend to process goals, outcomes will tend to take care of themselves. Goal-achievement strategies should include how players plan on accomplishing the short-term goals and improve upon their weaker areas in practice and games (e.g., through specific drills, actions, thoughts).

Another important aspect of setting goals is feedback, which is when SMART goals become so critical. SMART goals by nature provide internal feedback to the player. Was the goal accomplished? If not, what went wrong? External feedback from coaches is also critical to the goal-setting process. Players should set their own goals, but obtaining suggestions in terms of specific areas in need of attention is very important. Continual feedback from coaches in terms of goal progress (or goal revision) is also critical.

Figure 10-1. Setting SMART goals can help guide a team toward success.

The following examples highlight the use of SMART goals for setters and hitters:
- This week in practice I will improve my passing efficiency by completing 80% of my sets, while only overpassing one per 15 sets.
- I am going to improve my scanning of blocking coverages by watching extra game/practice video for 20 minutes before or after each practice.
- This week in practice I will improve my ability to let go of serving/hitting errors by practicing my pre-serve or pre-hitting routine before every swing during scrimmage.
- By next Friday, I will learn all of the new plays by having the coach test me for several minutes before and during each practice this week.

Players can learn from goals being accomplished ("Keep doing what I've been doing") and from those goals that are not being met ("Since what I'm doing is not working, what changes must be made?"). At this point, you can offer instruction on what needs to be changed. Having players and coaches monitor progress of predetermined goals is a valuable skill to utilize on a consistent basis. The more often coaches refer to these goals and reinforce any progress made toward accomplishing them, the more empowering they will become for the players.

"People must be able to understand...that if they identify with the team goal, their individual goals will be achieved."
—Mike Krzyzewski, Head Men's Basketball Coach, Duke University(Williams, 1997, p. 183)

One way to present individual or team goals to your players or team is to insert these goals onto a staircase diagram. The idea is for them to see that before they can proceed to the next stair, or goal, the previous goal needs to be accomplished. The goals nearer the bottom of the staircase can be pre-season goals, followed by the in-season goals, topped with some post-season goals. Figure 10-2 is an example of a goal staircase that follows these progressions for the entire team. These goals include both short- and long-range goals as well as process and outcome goals. This goal staircase can either be given to each player or posted in the locker room or in the practice gym. Moreover, these goal staircases can be specific to each position, since each positional unit will have their own standards and goals.

Figure 10-2. Short and long-range team goal staircase

Accountability

Continually referring back to goals, definitions, the team identity, and practice standards is critical to achieving lasting effects. Holding players accountable to these goals and standards is a little easier because the players helped to devise them. One of the better ways of keeping the players accountable to these standards is to have them rate their progress and evaluate what areas need continual improvement. Through continual evaluation and encouragement, as well as by allowing players the opportunity to voice their opinions on important team issues, can increase their sense of responsibility, ownership, and commitment to the team's efforts. One way of doing this is to have players rate their progress on each of the goals-standards on a scale of 1 to 10 (1 equals "no progress" and 10 equals a "total change for the better"). Obtaining a team average for each goal and standard can lead to an active discussion on what the team has done well—and not done well—to accomplish desired changes, as well as what needs to happen to continue the progress and improvement.

Courtesy of USC Sports Information

Figure 10-3. It is crucial for coaches to offer feedback regarding goal progress, and take full advantage of coachable moments to help reinforce team standards.

The key component of a goal-setting program is getting players to govern and police themselves with regards to team rules, standards, and communication procedures. Once this is accomplished, a team becomes "player driven" as opposed to "coach driven." Coach Marty Schottenheimer of the San Diego Chargers echoes this sentiment: "The most successful teams that I've been around were those where the players drove the machine" (Didenger, 1995).

Meeting regularly with players individually and the team as a whole, coupled with an open line of communication, allows players to voice their opinions in an open forum and gives each team member a say in the workings of the team. Keep in mind that players should be allowed to provide feedback and dialogue on team issues only (e.g., standards, goals, rules), not on playing time/status issues, scheduling, practice activities, or game strategy, all of which are reserved for the coaching staff. Coach Dennis Green of the Arizona Cardinals offers some good advice warning coaches about taking this feedback too far: "A common mistake made by some coaches is they let their superstars write their own rules" (*Los Angeles Times*, 2003c).

When teams or positional units are not able to challenge themselves to maintain the standards set by the team, then the coaches need to step in and dish out some sort of predetermined punishment. If the captains are not leading the way as needed, then new captains may need to be chosen. Starters who are not modeling the correct behaviors must become non-starters for a spell. The dishing out of punishment must be calculated and not done with haste; it takes time to find the right "buttons" to push to lead to behavior change. Making players do extra conditioning may make the coaches feel better but does it allow the team to grow closer as a unit? This punishment may work for some teams, but usually taking away responsibility and playing time speaks louder than a coach's whistle. Taking advantage of those "coachable moments" can really assist in developing a team mindset. Coachable moments include times when players make sacrifices for the greater good like hustling for another teammate, finishing off sprints to set good examples, not allowing other players to complain about a drill, or challenging teammates to give quality reps. So many coaches are too quick to point out when things are not working that they fail to take advantage of those moments when teams are clicking and playing as one.

"Being the best is a simple decision…It's not glamorous. It's not about glory or God-given talent. It's about commitment, plain and simple. But saying you want to be at the very top of your field and doing it are two different things. The bottom line is, if I don't go into it every day consistently committed, I won't get results.
—Mia Hamm, Olympic/World Cup Champion soccer star
(Dorfman, 2003, p. 258)

A final note about accountability: Do not forget the importance of player commitment to the goals and standards of the team. Players who have a high level of commitment have already "bought what the team is selling" and will do what needs to be done for the team to be successful. Jeff Janssen, in his book, *Championship Team Building*, lists six different levels of commitment. These levels can be described as existing on a continuum, from the least committed, called the resistant phase, to the two highest degrees of commitment, committed and compelled. After reading through the definitions of each, ask yourself how many of your players fall into each category. The commitment continuum describes the following types of players:

- Resistant players are those who are on a different page than the rest of the team and are motivated by their own agenda.
- Reluctant players do enough to get by but are not truly on board.
- Existent players are driven by other motives that do not match those of the overall team, so the commitment level to the team goals suffers.
- Compliant players are those who do what is asked of them and understand the importance of collective action.
- Committed players are those who are not only compliant, but put in extra energy to help make the team succeed.
- Compelled players are those totally driven by the team's pursuit and do all they can to assist.

According to Janssen (2002), championship teams have most of their players in the "compliant" to "compelled" categories. Where are the majority of your players? Posting this commitment continuum on a board for the team to see and self-assess where they perceive themselves can be an interesting activity. Coaches can then compare where they thought each player was on the commitment continuum to where the player perceived himself to be. This chapter provides strategies for improving player commitment to the team pursuit.

> "When a team outgrows individual performance and learns team confidence, excellence becomes a reality."
> —Joe Paterno, Head Football Coach, Penn State Football
> (Williams, 1997, p. 8)

Team Communication

Effective team communication and teamwork are often taken for granted. What works with one team does not necessarily work for another. Breakdowns in communication—whether they exist from coach to player, player to player, or player to coach—are often the cause of conflict,. Ensuring that all parties are practicing effective communication techniques is essential for optimal teamwork and achievement on the court.

Team meetings should be conducted to learn more about communication issues, the consequences of ineffective communication, and ways to improve. Major topics to discuss include the importance of sending effective messages as well as receiving messages effectively (Figure 10-4).

Sending Effective Verbal Messages
- Be direct and specific
- Be clear and consistent
- Focus on one thing at a time
- Be consistent with what is being said and subsequent nonverbal messages
- Deliver messages immediately

Receiving Effective Verbal Messages
- Be an active listener (paying attention, giving appropriate feedback, and good nonverbal communication, e.g., eye contact)
- Be a supportive listener (value the speaker and the message)

Figure 10-4. Sending and receiving messages

"If you cannot relate (establish a relationship) to today's player, you're through as a coach."
— Steve Mariucci, Head Coach, Detriot Lions (Dorfman, 2003, p. 42)

It is important for players and coaches to be aware of the "external signs" they are emitting during practice or matches. These external signs consist of nonverbal cues, body language, posture, gestures, and facial expressions (rolling the eyes, looking away), all of which may be perceived as positive, negative, or neutral. Those behaviors perceived as neutral or negative are not conducive for open communication. Many players hurt themselves by not being aware of their nonverbal behaviors, especially in stressful times. A player can cast himself in a negative light if he shows too many negative nonverbal behaviors. The same can happen to coaches.

As Figure 10-4 shows, breakdowns in communication can occur due to faulty messages (either sending or receiving) via both verbal and nonverbal communication methods. Coaches who are cognizant of the verbal-nonverbal communication patterns of their team (player to player, player to coach, coach to player) will be in a better position to step in if the need arises and intervene appropriately. The most common consequences of ineffective communication are frustration, anger, dissatisfaction, withdrawal, derision between teammates, frequent confrontations, and the formation of cliques (teammates begin to take sides). These can be avoided if the team discusses the importance of effective communication practices, and how to improve upon team communication.

Communication standards set by coaches and their players should be evaluated in terms of team progress. As with any team, conflicts can occur throughout the season, but since time has been taken to establish communication standards, it will be easier to define the problems and suggest ways of correcting them. Teams that follow the "Ten Commandments" of communication (Anshel, 1990) help establish an excellent standard of open communication for their players and coaches. The list in Figure 10-5 has been modified to specifically address team communication practices for coaches and players.

Thou shalt
.....be honest and consistent
.....be a good listener
.....break out of comfort zones
.....be empathetic
.....never be sarcastic
.....be specific and productive with feedback
.....trust teammates and coaches
.....be able to productively challenge teammates
.....not allow teammates to drift
.....use productive nonverbal behaviors

Figure 10-5. "10 Commandments" for effective team communication

Being honest and consistent means telling players what they need to hear rather than what they want to hear. The fight against mediocrity is a taxing, constant battle that requires coaches who are willing to encourage, confront, and challenge players on a daily basis. The same goes for players who truly want to challenge each other to get better. This is a skill that may need to be taught to some players or teams.

This may sound a bit simplistic, but being a good listener means improving upon the skill of active listening. Allowing someone the opportunity to voice his opinions is hard for most, especially listening without judging or getting defensive. Being open to new and different ideas is a critical component of being an active listener. Doing so also means breaking out of comfort zones. Every team player must feel comfortable about speaking to the coach and his teammates if he has problems or issues to share. Players who are too quiet and shy do not get their opinions voiced, and therefore usually do whatever everyone else does. These players may be quite dissatisfied with an issue that will go unresolved due to their unwillingness to bring it up. Coaches are primarily responsible for creating a climate in which players have the ability to offer their insights without hesitation.

Another important means of improving team communication, particularly among the players, is empathy, or putting yourself in someone else's shoes via "trying on" their thoughts and feelings. Coaches who can also acknowledge the many variables impacting players' performance and well-being will be better prepared to help if needed.

Courtesy of Morgan Paige

Figure 10-6. USC players wear their team standards on the back of their training shirts, which serves to remind them what must be done daily.

Sarcastic feedback to players and teammates serves one purpose— beating down the player on the receiving end. Confidence gets hit hard by mindless sarcasm. Being critical is one thing; being sarcastic is another. Sarcasm should not be a part of anyone's arsenal of methods used to improve motivation, as it usually accomplishes exactly the opposite.

Coaches use two forms of constructive feedback, positive and productive feedback. Positive feedback ("you are a really good player") serves one purpose—to help players feel better about themselves. This may lead to increased confidence and improved performance. But competitive athletes want more than the "warm fuzzies." They want specific performance cues or teaching points, called productive feedback, regarding what worked and what did not work (and why). Being positive only gets players so far. Offering productive feedback gives detailed comments to athletes about their performance, rather than simply stroking their ego. There are usually enough people who "pump up" players' egos (family, friends), and more usually is not needed.

Trusting teammates and coaches means not having to question their beliefs, drive, commitment, work ethic, desire, expertise, and talent. A lot of the friction that occurs within a team stems from a lack of trust. Players doubting the decisions made by the coaching staff (treatment of players, playing time, play calling), and coaches believing that players are putting themselves before the team are two common situations that illustrate a lack of team trust. Once trust is established, players can then begin to productively challenge their teammates. In most cases, this means telling a teammate that he needs to give more to the team, such as more effort and a greater commitment. Yet once practice or games are over, friendships should still be intact. The ability to challenge teammates is more a matter of trust than it is about being assertive.

> *"I truly believe that when you're trying to find out who your true guys are, there are probably 20% that are winners, 20% that are losers, and 60% looking for direction. So you put the onus on them... It's accountability, responsibility, and trust. You trust that the guy next to you is doing his job, that he's doing his homework, that he's working the trade."*
> —George O'Leary, former NFL coach, now at Central Florida
> (USA Today, 2003, p. 2C)

If teams truly want to excel, helping each other push beyond individual comfort zones is a prerequisite. Caution must be given regarding the tone and delivery of this feedback, however. Being productive means providing useful information and a rationale for the feedback, not simply yelling at teammates (negative feedback). Also, be mindful of the use of productive nonverbal behaviors, since a lot can be told from how players carry themselves, especially in tough times. Finally, players cannot allow a teammate to drift or separate from the team due to frustrations with his own play (especially mistakes). Instead, they should help to bring him back into the mix through positive, productive encouragement, high fives, pats on the back, or even specific technical advice.

Figure 10-7. The content, delivery, and timing of feedback can be critical to team effectiveness.

"When a team is united, it won't make any difference what outsiders think... your competition will have fewer weaknesses to exploit. But a team divided against itself can break down at any moment. The least bit of pressure or adversity will crack it apart."
—Bill Parcells, Head Coach, Dallas Cowboys (Williams, 1997, p. 147)

Team-Bonding Activities

For years, coaches from all types of team sports have incorporated team bonding activities to complement their training sessions before the start of the season. One of the primary goals for these team-bonding activities is to help teammates to get to know each other and to begin to form bonds, so when the pressure of the season begins these bonds are tight enough for the team to persevere and thrive. This process is referred to as team cohesion. Team cohesion consists of two interactive components, task cohesion and social cohesion. Task cohesion reflects the ability of the team to work together toward common goals, while social cohesion refers to the closeness between teammates (Carron, Spink, & Prapavessis, 1997).

Figure 10-8. Having teams participate in team-bonding activities, like painting motivational messages in the practice gym, can go a long way to building social and task cohesion.

The ideal situation is for teams to be strong in both task and social cohesion. A team who likes hanging together off the field, as well as work hard together on the field, is in a better position to be successful. Teams that suffer from cliques, personality clashes, poor communication practices, and daily confrontations struggle with social cohesion. Poor social cohesion can obviously have a negative impact on how willing these players are to put in maximal, collective efforts on the field. Team-building intervention programs can help coaches and teams improve upon both components of cohesion. Specifically, taking players through goal-setting, standard-setting, and other brainstorming sessions can help players get on the "same page" and improve task cohesion, while team-bonding activities have been found to be effective in improving team social cohesion.

A *Sports Illustrated* article (McCallum, 2001) detailed how many top collegiate football programs incorporate team-building activities into their summer "voluntary" conditioning sessions, some even adopting the credo "bond in the heat and we can't be beat!" For example, University of Oregon players rafted down the Willamette River, while the Mississippi Bulldogs endured Army-like basic-training exercises. Other anecdotes included players from Louisiana State University taking part in karate training, and the Fighting Illinois playing in a football-players-only Wednesday night softball league. The Hokies from Virginia Tech hit several stops along the NASCAR circuit, while players from Texas Tech engaged in organized sparring sessions with local boxers. Although varied, these team-building activities were all organized to create a more closely knit team that would then (hopefully) lead to winning games in September. Some teams may go to a comedy club as a team, have a team bowling tournament, team movie night, pot-luck dinners, scavenger hunts, white water rafting trips, complete outdoor adventure courses, and go on camping outings. Coaches are only limited by their imagination.

"The trust we'll have in one another during the season will have been built in the summer, and there's no way you can overvalue trust on a football team."
   —Ryan Schmid, Center, University of Oregon (McCallum, 2001, p. 76)

Team-Building Implementation

Applying the six components described previously entails packaging them into a team-building intervention program. The following stages incorporate general implementation procedures and specific application strategies to a team-building intervention program that can be used for volleyball teams.

Stage One

A formal needs assessment is conducted by coaches who specifically attempt to answer the following question: What does this team need to do to be successful? Coaches should think in terms of the physical, technical, strategic, team, mental, emotional, and inspirational capacities, as discussed in Chapter 3.

Stage Two

Using this information, coaches develop a specific plan that addresses how they can get the team to improve upon these needs. Decisions made on the exact team-bonding activities and team-building meeting topics should be made at this time as well.

Stage Three

Conduct an initial team meeting between the team and coaches that consists of an educational orientation about what team building is and guidelines for optimal team communication. You can then facilitate brainstorming sessions on what this team needs to do to be successful. List comments from coaches and players on a blackboard. This would be an ideal time to have players think and record their primary motives for playing and specific preferences for coach and teammate behaviors and feedback.

Stage Four

The team prioritizes the input and then additional brainstorming is conducted to define each point and how it can be assessed and accounted for in action words. This is an important step because defining each strategy puts a "face on it." Another meeting point could include establishing a team identity.

Stage Five

Follow-up meetings can be conducted to develop short- and long-range goals, action plans that detail how these goals will be achieved, team rules, and standards of execution.

Stage Six

Follow-up meetings can include an evaluation of team progress on their standards and goals (via rating sheets and open discussions), and progress on team cohesion and team communication. It is absolutely critical to provide feedback and evaluation to the players for the intervention to have maximal effect.

Stage Seven

Team meetings can then be set up to deal with conflicts that may occur during the season, as well as incorporate some team-cohesion activities during the midst of the season, such as team meals and outings to continue to foster task and social cohesion.

Chapter Summary

- Effective teamwork can often be the difference between success and failure.
- A carefully designed team-building program is a proactive way to combat potential team barriers before they occur.
- Asking the team to identify their "team identity" is another method of obtaining player feedback regarding goals and motives, and how they would like to be seen by others.
- Setting SMART goals is recommended.
- Players can learn from goals being accomplished as well as from those that are not being met.
- Breakdowns in communication—from coach to player, player to player, or player to coach—are often the cause of conflicts.
- The fight against mediocrity is a taxing, constant battle that requires coaches willing to encourage, confront, and challenge players on a daily basis.
- Team-building intervention programs include brainstorming team motives/preferences, team identity, goals, methods of accountability, collaborative communication and trust, and team bonding activities, all designed to improve social and task team cohesion.

11

Applying Mental Toughness
Training to Everyday Coaching

It is first critical for coaches to realize that applying mental-toughness skills to their players is similar to presenting and teaching technical skills and play calls. Moreover, most coaches already present mental skills to their players and teams in their everyday coaching without even knowing it.

Everyday Application of Mental-Skill Strategies

Plenty of coaches appreciate the importance of the mental side of their sport and attempt to get this information across to their players. Others still feel that mental-skills training is too time consuming, should only be used with athletes in slumps or with only the most elite athletes, or is just not effective. The major aim of this section is to demystify mental skills training for those skeptic coaches out there, while also educating all coaches about fundamental ways of incorporating mental-skills training into their everyday coaching.

The five mental-skill methods that have been found to be important for consistent, optimal performance include imagery, goal setting, pre-performance routines, concentration training, and intensity regulation. Upon reading the following sections, ask yourself how many of these fundamental mental-skill methods are you presently using in your everyday coaching?

Courtesy of Oregon State Sports Information

Figure 11-1. Coaches should realize that they already teach the mental game to their teams.

Imagery

Use of imagery includes the following:
- Use of video breakdowns and highlight tapes (McCann, 2002)
- Use of scouting reports
- Walk-throughs of the competition site prior to playing
- Use of creative language that helps to give players a clearer "picture" to teach complex sports skills (McCann, 2002), like "sitting back" when in a passing-digging platform
- Walk-throughs of plays and strategies during practice
- Mentally rehearsing plays, routines, or technical drills before physically doing them
- Mentally picturing the court or large crowd the night before
- Modeling technical execution via seeing it, feeling it, and repeating it

All of these coaching strategies incorporate the use of imagery to aid in learning skills and tactics, preparation, and performance execution. If you use some or all of these methods, you have been teaching your players one of the key mental-skill methods. Chapter 12 offers more details as well as additional ways of incorporating imagery into your coaching.

Goal Setting

Helping athletes and teams set goals is an effective means of enhancing team building, team motivation, and process-oriented behavior. Goal setting includes the following:

- Giving players a verbal or written practice plan
- Giving players a verbal or written game plan
- Describing specific objectives for the week of practice, or at the beginning of each individual practice
- Targeting specific performance areas the team is in need of improving
- Conducting team meetings to discuss what is needed for the team to have a successful season
- Defining roles and responsibilities for each member of your team
- Continuously reminding players of areas they are in need of improving

Goal setting has been proven by research and reports from elite athletes to be effective in influencing performance by enhancing upon player motivation, self-confidence, commitment, effort, and mental readiness. Pursuing specific short-term goals on the way to achieving longer-term goals conveys reliable information to the athlete about their capabilities and their progress. When one is making progress toward a goal, confidence, commitment, and motivation increases.

Pre-performance Routines

At the elite level, where athletes possess similar sport-specific and physical abilities, the way athletes engage their thoughts and emotions before a competition could be the difference between winning and losing. When most players think about negative things and get down on themselves, they usually play their worst games, while those who keep themselves thinking productively and find ways of keeping themselves feeling good end up having their better performances. One of the most important factors contributing to top performances is the ability to generate and maintain optimal readiness prior to competition. One method of improving physical, mental, and emotional readiness is through the use of pre-performance routines. The following list details the many ways that you may already be utilizing preparatory routines in your coaching.

- Establishing a schedule for pre-game activities, such as meetings, meals, treatment, and dressing
- Establishing a schedule for pre-practice activities
- Allowing players some "free" time before the game for personal preparation activities
- Teaching servers pre-serve routines to use just prior to execution
- Walking through specific warm-up activities to ensure effective execution

- Using pre-game pep talks to energize the squad
- Giving players individualized feedback prior to games to energize, relax, motivate, increase confidence, or instruct

All these preparatory strategies incorporate many different components, including motivational components (pep talks), technical aspects (pre-game coaching points), and attempts at enhancing confidence, coping with anxiety, improving concentration, and increasing readiness. Several methods are presented later in this chapter that players can utilize to develop their own pre-performance routines.

Concentration Training

Attentional focus is the ability to focus on the most relevant information during play. Attentional switching is the ability to adjust one's attentional focus (width and direction) depending upon the particular sport situation. Concentration training includes the following:

- Instructing players on specific performance cues
- Offering coaching points to players during games that direct them toward specific technical or strategic elements of play
- Offering coaching points to players during practices that direct them toward specific technical or strategic elements of play
- Calling time-outs to help players focus on important elements of the next play
- Using simulation training, such as piping in crowd noise or the use of visual distractions, during practice to prepare players for game-like conditions
  Calling time-outs in an attempt to "freeze" the opponent's server prior to a big point

Instructing players to focus on certain performance cues and execute without thought or hesitation are two ways that you can teach players how to alter their concentration style to match the particular situation. When coaches call time-outs to "freeze" opponents, it is their intention to force the server to become so internally focused (e.g., worry over the miss, think too much about the importance of the serve) that they miss because of all the mental interference.

Intensity Regulation

Gaining control over the level of intensity is one of the most important things athletes can do to improve upon their practice and game readiness (mental toughness). Levels of intensity are specific to each athlete. Some athletes perform better when they have low levels of intensity (very relaxed), while others need a moderate level (a composed intensity), and still others need a high level of intensity (pumped up!). Intensity regulation includes the following:

- Using pre-game pep talks to "pump up" the squad

- Instructing players to stay composed rather than letting their emotions take over; for example, telling players to not "lose control" when plays go against them or when they experience other adversities (e.g., perceived injustice, such as lack of playing time)
- Attempting to predict which players are nervous and which are too relaxed based upon "outward signs" and body language. Some coaches believe that every player needs to be pumped up to be ready to play, so they look for behaviors and actions that indicate that mental state.
- Telling players to "relax" when you perceive them to be uptight and nervous

Being able to relax is an important mental skill that some coaches just assume their players have. Realizing that each player differs in terms of their preference for intensity level, coaches must work with each player to figure out what level works best for him.

How many of these mental-skill strategies have you incorporated with your players and team? To those who utilize a great number of these fundamental methods, congratulations. You have been implementing some critical mental-skill strategies for the betterment of your players and teams. Coaches who are not utilizing these strategies are missing out on some great opportunities to improve upon their players' preparation and execution skills. All coaches can challenge themselves further by implementing additional mental-skill methods as described in Chapter 12.

Chapter Summary

- Most coaches already incorporate mental skills into their everyday coaching without even knowing it.
- The five mental-skill methods important for consistent, optimal performance are imagery, goal setting, pre-performance routines, concentration training, and intensity regulation.
- Coaches who are not utilizing many of the mental-skill strategies mentioned are missing some great opportunities to improve upon their players' preparation and execution skills.

12

Training for Automaticity IV: Combating Mental-Inspirational Barriers

> *"Free your mind, let it all go; fear, doubt, disbelief."*
> —Morpheus to Neo ("Mr. Anderson") in The Matrix

This chapter offers specific training strategies that players can utilize to effectively combat information and sequencing errors (thus freeing their minds), so that they can automatically execute the skills needed at game-time. These same strategies can be utilized to combat other mental, emotional, and inspirational performance barriers.

Strategies include tough *thinking/talking, confidence/trust training, intensity mastery/training, concentration training,* and *physical/mental preparation-readiness.* These strategies are not only clearly defined in this chapter, but specific activities and examples for implementing these strategies are also included for easy application by coaches and players.

Tough Thinking and Talking

Being able to "master" inner dialogue and thoughts takes more than just "thinking positively." How players (and coaches) think and talk to themselves can enhance or hurt performance. Athletes who are more aware of their thoughts and self-talk, and who also develop plans for dealing with inappropriate and damaging thoughts and talk, are more consistent performers and perform better in pressure situations. Thinking and talking tough are two difficult things, especially in pressure situations (speaking in front of class, playing in the title game, taking exams, swinging for game point).

Tough thinking and talking requires productive thoughts prior to and during games. Productive thoughts and talk help players perform better via performance cues such as "soft hands" or "quick swing." Counter to productive thoughts are the negative, self-defeating ones such as: "I can't play with this team" or "I am not good at hitting high sets." Negative thoughts and talk are also referred to as "stinking thinking."

"Coaches should encourage in players the self-talk 'I can' and 'I will' because what they look for, what they expect to see, what they believe is possible is what they are likely to discover. A phrase such as 'I'm trying' does not provide clarity and the confident mindset that pushes people to get better."

—Jona Braden, Head Volleyball Coach, Kentucky
(*The Volleyball Coaching Bible*, 2002, p. 38)

Self-statements and thoughts serve numerous purposes. For one, they help direct attention in terms of what specific cues players find themselves focusing on and whether these are advantageous to performance. Secondly, a player may use self-dialogue to label himself, his teammates, or his opponents, such as "I am a choker," or "the D.S. is too tough tonight for me to find seams." Finally, these statements and thoughts are used to judge performances, such as "that was a great angle kill." As previously stated, these statements and thoughts can really help or destroy mental toughness and automatic, consistent execution.

Common Types of Negative Thinking

Worrying over Future Events

When thoughts are focused too much on the future ("what if I... don't put away this set... lose this game"), focus on the present play will suffer greatly. Attentional capacities are limited, so worrying over future events will leave little attentional capacity for present performance. In most cases, what players worry over, such as not making the play or looking foolish because of a bad mistake, will usually occur due to the self-fulfilling prophecy. What this is, simply stated, is the body following the lead set by thoughts and self talk. Since thoughts govern action, if a player is thinking that he is going to set a bad set, his body will follow. However, if this player honestly believes that he is going to set a perfect set, unless something changes in the environment, such as solid blocking coverage, or a poor pass from a teammate, he has a much greater chance of doing just that. So many players sabotage their performances before they even step out onto the court. (Refer to Chapter 9 for examples of mental misses.)

Fretting over Mistakes

Fretting over mistakes means an individual is playing in the past. Players cannot go back and change what has happened no matter how much they would like to do so. Players can only learn from the past and move on to the next opportunity. Since attentional capacities are limited, it is important to solely play in the present. Using a refocusing routine after making a mistake will help a player stop replaying the mistake over and over again, which usually results in him carrying the mistake to the next play or plays.

Worrying over the Uncontrollables

Almost everyone worries about things out of their control—the "uncontrollables"—such as weather, traffic, and long lines in restaurants. Athletes do the same thing in terms of worrying about not making mistakes, worrying over opponent's play, worrying over what coaches are thinking, and worrying over outcome. Even the play during games is an uncontrollable—your team has no control over how the opponent will play. All players can do is make it as difficult as possible for opponents to play to their fullest potential. Helping players identify what they do and do not have control over is a good place to start. Players (and coaches) need to realize that if they have no control over a situation, they should let it go and refocus on things that they can control, like their preparation and execution. See Chapter 12, Figure 12-8, for a chart that players can complete to help them acquire this skill.

Fretting over Weaknesses during a Game

Ideally, while competing, players should be on "automatic" player and simply read and react to the ever-changing game situations. Yet, many players really struggle with "freeing the mind" and just playing. So if players need to have a couple of thoughts or statements in their heads, it is the coach's job to ensure that they are productive in nature. Productive thoughts and self-talk should include technical or strategic cues that improve play, such as "getting into position quicker on the next play," or "the block keeps stepping early to the ball," or even motivational talk, such as "let that one go and get ready for the next play." If players are thinking and evaluating about how poorly they are playing, their play will only worsen. Maintaining a clear mind or using productive cues is not easy—it takes practice.

Focusing Too Much on Winning

Despite the fact that most players compete to win, when it becomes the sole reason for playing they are setting themselves up for failure. Players and coaches must understand that winning is a process, and that if players don't work on the process of playing well, winning will not happen unless the team gets lucky or plays against a lesser opponent. Players should be thinking of ways to play better and help the team rather than just about winning the game. Also, opponents have a lot to do with whether teams win or not, so winning is somewhat of an uncontrollable. Coaches can begin to change this mindset by stressing game execution (how are we going to win?) rather than simply focusing on beating the opponent. The focus should always be on taking care of business on your own side of the net. This is what the players have total control over—their preparation and execution.

Figure 12-1. To win consistently, players must focus on the process—improving every practice, every game

Fretting over Being Perfect

Another uncontrollable is trying to be perfect. No one is that good, and so much is beyond a player's control. *Striving* to be perfect is a sign of a true competitor, but *expecting* to be perfect is a sign of inappropriate and irrational thinking that sets an athlete up for failure on a daily basis. This type of thinking can also erode motivation and confidence.

Techniques to Develop Tough Thinking and Talking

Being a tough thinker and talker takes practice. Players can use exercises such as awareness training, thought stopping, restructuring, visualization, and self-coaching statements to help improve in this area. Each of these techniques is addressed in this chapter.

Do your players know what does and does not work for them? To find out, have them complete Figure 12-2. Players who are unaware of what works for them (i.e., those who cannot identify these simple, self-reflections) are at a disadvantage because they first need to improve upon their awareness abilities before sharpening their

Identify the most common negative thoughts that enter into your head before/during games	Identify the most common negative self-statements you say to yourself before/during games
(1)	(1)
(2)	(2)
(3)	(3)
(4)	(4)
List a productive thought to replace the negative statement listed above	List a productive self-statement to replace the negative statement listed above
(1)	(1)
(2)	(2)
(3)	(3)
(4)	(4)

Figure 12-2. Identifying tough thoughts and talk

mental skills. Players who at least know some of what they are thinking and saying before, during, and after play are in a position to change their mindset to positives rather than negatives. When most athletes think about negative things and get down on themselves, they usually play their worst games. On the flip side, those who keep thinking productively and find ways to feel composed end up having their better performances. Thinking positively is easy when a player is playing well—it is a different story when things are not going so well. It is called mental toughness for a reason—it is tough to think this way consistently, especially during tougher times when things are not going the athlete's way.

Once players have identified the most common negative thoughts and self-statements they say to themselves before and during games, and they replace them with productive thoughts and self-statements, the next step entails believing in the productive statements and not the negative ones. Players do this by "building a case" for why these productive thoughts and self-statements are true.

- Example 1: "I really am a good player because I made this top team and I play a lot."
- Example 2: "I want to be the player with the ball in my hands in the final minutes because I have done so in the past and won the game with a big play."
- Example 3: "My coach and my teammates will still respect me even if I make mistakes."
- Example 4: "I don't have to worry about making mistakes because everyone makes mistakes and they are necessary to become the best player I can be."

Keep in mind that some athletes can be pretty good about keeping themselves positive and productive, but even these athletes need to work on their mental toughness and mechanics. In times of big-time pressure (championship game, big exam), athletes who have not practiced these skills may choke under the pressure if they've begun to listen to and believe the negative thoughts and talk that have seeped in.

Confidence and Trust Training

Confidence is an inner belief that certain tasks can be accomplished. Top performers from all sports have been found to be very confident about their performances. They do not doubt their abilities, but rather believe that every time out on the court they can and will play well. Athletes who are able to think this way do not let their play dictate their confidence. Rather, their confidence level remains high and consistent, thereby dictating their performance (e.g., high confidence equals top performance).

Figure 12-3. Playing in front of large crowds can cause some players to choke under the perceived pressure.

Confidence is similar to trust. Athletes who are trusting of their abilities do not doubt their physical, technical, and tactical skills, or their mental mechanics, because they know that that in times of need (big plays), they will perform well and these skills will get the job done. When athletes begin to lose trust in their abilities, via negative talk or thoughts, their levels of anxiety and muscle tension increase, causing an overnarrowing of attention that causes some players to miss important performance cues. Some players will even change their mechanics in an attempt to get back on track, such as forcing plays, aiming, or controlling the passes or swing. Later in this chapter, the concept of trust and its potential impact on mechanics, in addition to strategies to combat this occurrence, is discussed further.

Confidence has been described as an "inverted U" process. As Figure 12-4 indicates, most players do not perform optimally when their level of confidence is low, yet as their confidence increases, so does the level of play. Yet once their confidence heightens to a level of "overconfidence," performance will begin to wane. Players who begin to assume that they will come up with great plays at will are the same ones who stop doing what they did to achieve their level of success (e.g., worked hard, focused on the process, led the team through solid play and encouragement). Arrogance often replaces the "little things," the intangibles that helped these players achieve. So when the time comes that the successes are not as common, these same players may turn on coaches and teammates (i.e., blame them for his failures) and drift further away from the "ingredients" that made them stand out and succeed. Players who are able to maintain a consistently high level of confidence, regardless of performance outcome, are giving themselves the best chance at succeeding come game time.

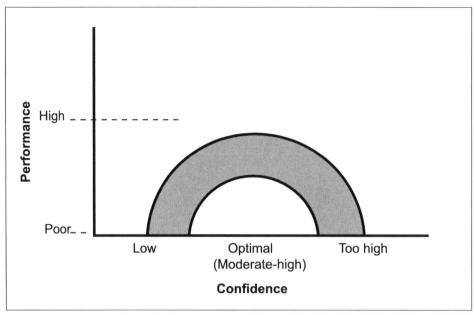

Figure 12-4. Inverted U confidence model

To assist those players in need of improving their confidence, have them begin the process by completing the lists in Figure 12-5. Next, have players come up with statements that reflect these same positive attitudes and thoughts about themselves and their abilities. These positive statements are referred to as self-coaching statements and should express personal, sometimes motivational, messages. Figure 12-6 offers a chart in which to record these statements. Some examples include the following:

- "I really come through in pressure situations—I am our team's go-to player!"
- "I'm the one who really wants the ball when the game is on the line."
- "I love playing in big games."
- "I feel like in any situation I can come up with a big play."

Positive Qualities	Successes
(1)	(1)
(2)	(2)
(3)	(3)
(4)	(4)
(5)	(5)

Figure 12-5. Confidence-building statements

Self-Coaching Statements
*
*
*
*
*
*
*

Figure 12-6. Self-coaching statement chart

Now that the players have some feel-good, productive, and motivating self-coaching statements, what do they do with them? Players should find creative ways to use them as often as possible. Some ideas you can suggest for how players can make the most of the statements that work best for them are listed here.

- Choose one or two statements each day to repeat over and over, especially prior to playing.
- Write the statement on paper many times throughout the day, with the idea in mind that the more you tell yourself these statements, the more that you will really believe them.
- Post these statements in a folder to read over when you have a few spare moments.
- Post them somewhere in your room so you see them many times throughout the day.
- Write them down and put them in your sport bag, so when you put on your equipment and uniform you can review them before and after practice or games.
- Record the statements on audiotape or compact disc, along with some of your favorite music and play them whenever you can, especially before practice and games.
- Visualize highlights from past successful performances or mentally picture future match play.

Taking advantage of the many sources of performance confidence can be a tremendous way to optimize player confidence. You should attempt to refer to these many sources when you address your players. For example, during pre-game talks, highlight your players' preparation (watching the tape of the opponent), emphasize the use of an individual and/or team highlight tape (previous success), remind players that they have run the rotations all week (mastery), and have organized pre-game routines to follow (mental preparation). The following sources of confidence have been identified by a sport psychology researcher, Robin Vealey (2002):

- Previous accomplishments—watching previous successes on video
- Vicarious experience—gaining confidence and energy by watching teammates' successes or watching or reading about the accomplishments of athletes from other sports
- Communication—openly and honestly communicating goes a long way in helping players and teammates feel appreciated and valued
- Physical presentation—looking the part (outside-in training) and not showing what is really going on inside
- Physical preparation—working as hard as possible in training and conditioning
- Mental preparation—realizing the importance of the mental game and doing something about it via establishing routines and different ways of preparation, readiness, and coping
- Situational favorableness—gaining something positive and motivating from the site of the competition; for example, playing well there last time, or a good "look" or "feel" about it
- Leadership—a sense that when it comes "crunch time," the team leaders, coaches, or captains will lead the way
- Mastery attempts—appreciating efforts at improving the overall game and acknowledging success in these areas; attempting to improve upon yesterday's performance
- Quality training—knowing the difference between quality training sessions and going through the motions, then actively ensuring that quality sessions prevail

In addition to utilizing these sources of confidence in your feedback to players, make players aware of these sources and have them attempt to utilize them pre- and post-game. Players who are able to leave practices and especially games with several "kudos" or things that they did well (or positive feedback received from coaches and teammates) will increase their level of internal confidence. Most competitive athletes leave games thinking and harping on their mistakes and bad moments of play. Teaching players to learn from these errors and leave them behind will make them better prepared, more confident, and ready for the next practice and game. Additionally, players should be encouraged to "deposit" this confidence-enhancing feedback into their internal confidence "bank" via writing them down or reciting them as a pre-game routine. Maintaining an optimal level of confidence in good times and in bad takes conscious work. As stated previously, thinking in this fashion may not be easy, but that is why it is called mental "toughness."

Figure 12-7. Coaches can greatly improve player confidence by utilizing the many sources of confidence during and after practice and game play.

Courtesy of USC Sports Information

Intensity Mastery and Training

The ability to handle pressure, and the emotional reaction to pressure, is referred to as intensity control. Gaining control and mastery over intensity is one of the most important things players and coaches can do to improve upon practice and game readiness. Levels of intensity are specific to each athlete. Some athletes perform better when they have low levels of intensity (very relaxed), while others need a moderate level (a composed intensity), while still others need a high level of intensity (wired).

Once in their state of optimal intensity, players become more motivated, confident, focused, and ready. To determine what his optimal intensity is, each player should determine what works best for him. Have players think in terms of three distinct things:

- What do you *feel* physically (tense muscles? rapid breathing? rapid heart rate?)
- What are your *behaviors* before games? Some players like to sit by themselves and listen to tunes, others like to hang with teammates, while others like to buzz around the locker room and pace.
- What do you *think* about prior to the serve? Are you worried about how you or the team will play or are you thinking confidently? Are you too focused on the outcome (winning) or on the process of playing your game?

Players who are aware of what works for them will be better able to control their intensity levels, especially in pressure-packed situations, than those who have not a clue about their mental and emotional states. One way players can improve their awareness is to have them complete the checklist that follows, which lists common reactions to overintensity. Players are asked to put a check mark next to the symptoms they commonly experience.

Overintensity

Symptoms of Overintensity

- Physical: _____ muscle tension; _____shortened breathing; _____excessive sweating; _____nausea; _____cold extremities; _____increase in blood pressure and heart rate
- Behavioral: _____increase in pace during competition; _____bracing muscles (e.g., shoulders up to the ears); _____increase in superstitious behaviors; _____quickly agitated; _____loss of coordination; _____choke in performance or evaluative situations
- Mental: _____negative self-talk and thoughts; _____irrational thinking; _____overnarrowing of concentration; _____inability to let go of mistakes; _____feeling of uncontrollability
- Emotional: _____feeling of fear of making mistakes, embarrassment, or letting others down

Causes of Overintensity

- A lack of confidence ("stinking thinking" and self-talk)
- Focusing on the outcome (winning), or on being the best player on the court rather than enjoying the process
- Cracking under the weight of the expectations of others—namely parents, teammates, or coaches—or of unrealistic goals
- An unfamiliarity with certain situations and places, such as arriving late to the game site, or playing a new role or a new system
- Unexpected events, like having to play with a cold, with a nagging injury, or without the team leader
- Continual worry over the uncontrollables, things that most people believe they have control over but actually do not. For example, some athletes get so worried about what their coaches think of them that it distracts them and could adversely affect their play.

An exercise to help players enhance their awareness of what they do and do not have control over is depicted in Figure 12-8. It is important for athletes to not waste valuable mental energy and limited attentional capacity on worrying or fretting over those things beyond their immediate control. Athletes who are prone to this excess concern over the uncontrollables will have a decreased sense of control, waning confidence, and overintensity issues.

Controllables	Uncontrollables
Ex. 1: my workrate at practice	Ex. 1: calls made by officials
Ex. 2: if not pleased with something, can go and talk to coach	Ex. 2: decisions regarding playing time and play calling by my coach
*	*
*	*
*	*
*	*
*	*
*	*

Figure 12-8. The controllables and the uncontrollables

Underintensity

When players struggle with being underintense for games, their performances can suffer as well. Underintensity is characterized by low energy levels, little motivation and drive, and an attentional focus that is so broad that important performance cues go unnoticed. The symptoms of underintensity can include:

- Physical—being lethargic; low heart rate (resting heart rate); low energy
- Behavioral—decrease in "sharpness" during play; looking "slow" and being a "step-too-late"; poor performance
- Mental—react more to distractions; loss of motivation to give maximal effort; difficulty narrowing attentional focus to the important details of performance and the opponents

Causes of Underintensity

- Fatigue from a lack of rest and recovery between games, practices, school, and social activities

- Sleeping difficulties
- Poor eating/nutritional habits
- Lack of adequate hydration
- Nagging injuries left untreated
- Lack of motivation and drive (e.g., playing an opponent the team has beaten numerous times before)
- Being overconfident, such as "we can beat this team on our worst day"

Overconfidence is one reason why upsets happen all the time in sport, because players begin to feel that they can put in a "half-effort" and still accomplish the outcome (winning). This is one of the big problems associated with a team that is too outcome-oriented. A process-oriented team will attempt to improve upon its last performance regardless of the opponent. It has been said that the "great ones," like Jordan, Tiger, Gretzky, Montana, Clemens, Rice, and Elway, were driven to perform better than they did during the previous game. What a tough challenge for these truly exceptional competitors!

Strategies to Decrease Intensity

Mastering intensity levels entails being able to lower a player's intensity when you perceive that he is too amped and excited, as well as being able to increase intensity levels when a player is bored or unmotivated. When players struggle with overintensity, assist them with the following strategies.

Understanding the Causes of Overintensity

The first question players should attempt to answer is how these feelings of overintensity affect their feelings, thoughts, and performances. Some athletes tend to get "too much in their heads" (mental) by getting so negative about their games, while others tend to get overly "tight and tense," signaling physical tension in places that can adversely affect performance. Very few volleyball skills can be performed well when the muscles are tensed up. Still others experience a combination of these. To effectively lower intensity levels to an optimal level, ensure that if players are "too much in the head" they incorporate mental strategies, but if players are too "tight and tense" they practice physical relaxation strategies. Players who experience a combination of the two should incorporate strategies from both categories. Performance strategies are included here so coaches can better assist their players with their handling of intensity.

Physical Strategies

Releasing tension through a physical warm-up routine followed by stretching can be quite beneficial. Practicing tension-relaxation cycles is also advisable to educate players on distinguishing differences between feelings of relaxation and tension. In down times, such as before going to bed or before practice, making a fist tight (tension) then releasing and opening up the fingers and feeling the tension run out of the fingers will help to clarify feelings of relaxation. Have players continue this cycle numerous times until the hands feel totally relaxed after the tension cycle. This tension-relaxation cycle can be conducted with any muscle group that harbors muscle tension.

It does take practice to self-induce relaxation during games, so it is recommended that players spend some time every day to practice the technique. Some elite athletes prefer to do a head-to-toe tension-relaxation cycle, moving from one muscle group to the next. This technique is referred to as progressive relaxation. The more aware players are of the feelings of tension and relaxation, the quicker they can respond to release the tension in the heat of competition.

The next skill strategy used to regulate intensity levels is breathing. When players are extremely anxious and/or tense, they may respond to this intensity with shortened, irregular breathing patterns. Without adequate oxygen, players become fatigued because the cardiovascular and muscular systems do not work as efficiently as is needed and performance is affected.

> *"Before an important shot, I relax myself by taking a long, deep breath."*
> —Tiger Woods (2001, p. 265)

It is very important that athletes replenish their oxygen supply, simply by inhaling through the nose for a four-count. The belly should push out as a sign that there is enough air being taken in and that it is getting deep enough into the lungs. Have players then exhale through the mouth for a four-count, and focus on feeling any tension in the muscles and body with each exhaled breath. Some athletes will tense a muscle group with each inhalation, and then relax the muscle on each exhalation for a combined relaxation effect.

Mental Strategies

Prior to game time, if players feel anxious, it is important for them to discontinue focusing on their debilitating thoughts and self-dialogue. Rather, encourage players to engage themselves in conversations with teammates or listen to music, which will provide a much-needed distraction. Once these feelings have subsided, players can begin to prepare for the upcoming game. Coaches must allow for individual pre-game time because every player differs in how he gets himself ready. If players are not given their own time, this could lead to more anxiety and counteract the coach's methods of getting the team "up" and ready for games. Most coaches allow at least 30 minutes for player pre-game time.

Another strategy you may try is to avoid telling players during games to "relax." If players do not know how to relax, this statement will hurt rather than help them. What occurs in some situations is that once athletes hear that command, they get even more anxious because they realize that they must be emitting some obvious "nervous behaviors" to prompt their coach to yell that out to them. One of the first things players can do to alleviate these threatening thoughts or anxieties is to try to perceive the impending situation or competition as non-threatening. This skill is called *reframing*. Instead of thinking of the upcoming game as an extremely nerve-racking situation, have them view it instead as a challenge. What normally accompanies negative perceptions are negative thoughts, avoidance thoughts and practices (just wanting to get it over with or skipping out), or negative feelings and tight muscles.

Being a competitor means embracing situations in which you have to be at your best to succeed. Teaching players to seek out challenges rather than escape from potentially stressful situations is valuable. Enabling players to stay productive and positive instead of turning negative ("I can't play well against this team") can really go a long way. It is a lot easier said than done, however. The key is for players to be aware of when they are turning negative with their thoughts and self-dialogue—and then stop. Replacing these negative, self-defeating thoughts and talk with productive comments— "I played well last week so there should be no reason why I can't bring my "A" game against these guys"—can help players change their way of thinking and become consistent, productive thinkers. It is advisable for players to write down their most common negative thoughts and self-talk, then replace these with productive statements (see Figure 12-1). After repeating this process for several weeks, players will begin to utilize more productive statements. If negative thoughts break through, they will be replaced with helpful, constructive comments.

Performance Strategies

Coaches should promote familiarity with game situations by attempting to simulate game conditions and specific game situations in practice. Preparing for all of the unexpected situations that could arise before and during games is a valuable exercise for coaches and players.

Coaches and their players must also keep errors in proper perspective. Once players begin to worry about the negative consequences of their mistakes, which could include verbal harassment by coaches, fans, and parents, they will begin to press, aim, and control their movements. All of these adjustments are all potentially detrimental to optimal, consistent performance.

Coaches who avoid overemphasizing outcome (winning, records, "must-win" situations) to their players will help them to stay more process- focused (e.g., working toward improving their play rather than on just getting the result). Chapter 14 goes into greater detail about coaching with a process focus. As mentioned earlier, players can only control their own efforts and play, not the play of others, so winning is somewhat of an uncontrollable. A team may have their best outing of the season yet still lose due to a bad officiating call or a missed serve, or any one of hundreds of incidents that could stand in the way of the win. What is most productive for players is to emphasize the process, or what they need to do prior to, during, and after plays to help lead their team to victory.

Taking this "process" approach helps players to take one play at a time. Sometimes players need to adopt a "fake it until you make it" moniker to be able to move past a poor play or run of points. In pressure situations, when players may become quite nervous (several mistakes in a row, receiving serve at game point), acting and looking cool, calm, and composed can get translated by the "software" (brain impulses, thoughts, muscles) as meaning that everything is alright, so players can simply go for it. This has been referred to as *outside-in training* (Loehr, 1994). Players basically do something on the outside, such as physical presentation, acting, and behaviors, that gets translated as a good thing on the inside via thoughts and emotions. One of the simplest strategies players and coaches can do on the "outside" that has an unbelievable effect on the "inside" is smiling. Smiling releases chemicals into our system that are linked to feelings of happiness and relaxation.

Finally, *inside-out training* (Loehr, 1994) occurs when players think productively and positively about their abilities and their chances of success on the inside, which gets translated by the body as a positive, energizing message. This sharpens outside performances such as jumping, swinging, setting, passing, reaction time, and power, to help the athlete function optimally. The strategies contained in this book contain both outside-in (physical toughness-technical training) and inside-out (mental, emotional toughness) training programs.

Strategies to Increase Intensity

When players are not amped enough and are in need of a jump start, numerous ways of increasing intensity levels are available.

Physical Strategies

Intense activity, such as a sharp pre-game warm-up, is one of the most effective physical strategies to employ when the team is just lethargic. Physical activity that is sport-specific is desirable, but in the off-season, cross-training activities such as playing other sports or utilizing different conditioning activities can be very beneficial. As mentioned earlier, "fake it until you make it" can help in this case as well. When players act as if they are totally invested in the upcoming game they not only help their teammates get more "into it," but may have the same effect on each individual player.

Mental Strategies

Having players listen to their favorite upbeat tunes can help get them more "into" practice, lifting, conditioning, or game-play. Another strategy that is widely used by elite athletes from most sports is the use of *mental imagery*. Imagery is mentioned several times in this book because this skill strategy can be used to increase confidence, motivation, preparation, and readiness, and decrease intensity. Utilizing mental imagery can be very effective in improving drive and energy, especially when a player visualizes energizing images and past performance accomplishments. A quick-reference tutorial on imagery, found in Figure 12-9, will assist players in getting started with this skill strategy.

Imagery Tutorial

Step 1: Go to a quiet place where you can relax and not be disturbed.

Step 2: Select a variety of scenes and develop them with rich detail, including colors, sounds, smells, and feelings if possible (your bedroom, favorite class, scenes of your dog playing...).

Step 3: Select sport-specific images and include as much detail as possible.

Step 4: Practice visualizing people (teammates, fans, parents) into the scenes.

Step 5: Imagine being in a specific sport situation, either in the past (replay), or in a future event. Bring in as much detail as possible. Also feel yourself experiencing success in these scenes.

Step 6: When you get proficient at your visualization, you can then try to replay negative events so you can edit them the way you really wanted them to turn out. Being able to fix these negative events may help in ensuring that they don't get repeated, while also helping to increase confidence and decrease anxiety about these specific sport situations.

Step 7: It is highly recommended that you visually practice specific sport skills and game-related situations, especially those that may be giving you some problems, as often as possible.

Figure 12-9. Imagery tutorial

Players can visualize performing a skill or replay a particular event in one of two ways. From an *internal perspective*, the skill is viewed from inside the "mind's eye." Players should actually see and feel the volleyball in their hands after a set, for example. During this type of imagery, the brain is sending messages to the muscles as if the player is actually passing, digging, or serving the ball. From an *external perspective*, players watch themselves as a spectator would, or watch themselves play on television or video. Internal imagery is more effective according to some research, though the external approach is still effective at helping improve confidence, motivation, and intensity regulation.

One final exercise can assist players in finding their optimal intensity zone (Figure 12-10). As mentioned earlier, some players perform better when they have high levels of intensity, others prefer moderate levels, and some operate better at lower levels. To help players find their zone, which represents the perfect level of intensity for them, have them rate and record their pre-game intensity level from 1 (not intense at all) to 10 (highest intensity). The next step is to have them rate their performance after each game from 1 (played awful) to 10 (ESPN highlight!). After monitoring a few games, players should be able to see a pattern, and discover the level of intensity that is needed for them to perform at their best.

Pre-game Intensity Level	Performance Rating
game 1 =	game 1 =
game 2 =	game 2 =
game 3 =	game 3 =
game 4 =	game 4 =
game 5 =	game 5 =
Describe what your zone is like.	Zone =_____
Describe your feelings, thoughts, behaviors.	

Figure 12-10. Finding the intensity zone

Attentional Focus and Competitive Concentration

The majority of coaches have players who struggle with intensity issues, and who have difficulty keeping their attentional focus on what is really important. Similar to the scenario mentioned earlier in this chapter regarding perceived tension/anxiety, it is common to hear coaches yell out to players "stay focused out there" or, another favorite, "keep your head in the game." Without realizing it, while these coaches are identifying the problem, they are also contributing more pressure and stress, which only makes the problem even worse. This is especially true for those players who thought they were really focusing, but since the coach said something to the contrary they then think that the coach must have seen something indicating that their concentration must truly be "off."

Courtesy of SCVC & Ralf's Photography

Figure 12-11. Attending to the proper cues and concentrating on the ball are crucial mental skills for blockers.

The following are some important terms in understanding attentional focus. Figure 12-12 (Nideffer, 1976; 1989) depicts the many types of attentional focus.

• Attentional focus—an athlete's ability to focus on the most relevant information during play

- Concentration—the mental skills involved in keeping one's focus on the most relevant performance cues
- Attentional style—the preferred style of focusing on the sport environment
- Attentional switching—the ability to adjust attentional focus, width, and direction, depending upon what is required in certain situations

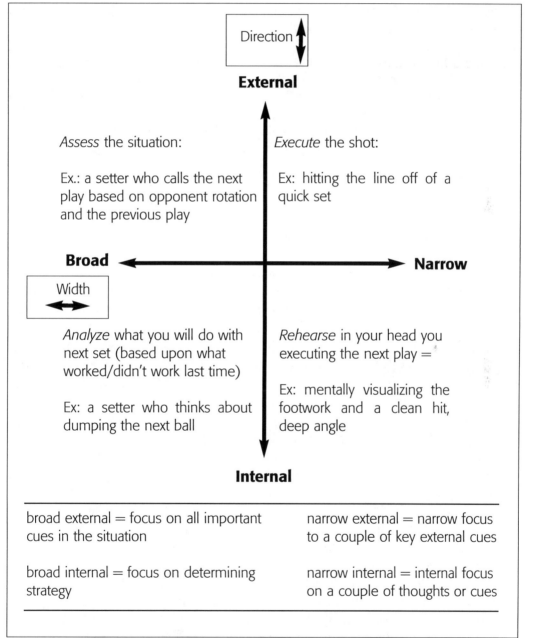

Direction

External

Assess the situation:

Ex.: a setter who calls the next play based on opponent rotation and the previous play

Execute the shot:

Ex: hitting the line off of a quick set

Broad ←→ **Narrow**

Width

Analyze what you will do with next set (based upon what worked/didn't work last time)

Ex: a setter who thinks about dumping the next ball

Rehearse in your head you executing the next play =

Ex: mentally visualizing the footwork and a clean hit, deep angle

Internal

broad external = focus on all important cues in the situation	narrow external = narrow focus to a couple of key external cues
broad internal = focus on determining strategy	narrow internal = internal focus on a couple of thoughts or cues

Figure 12-12. Components of attentional focus

- Width of attention—can range on a continuum:
  - ✓ Narrowing—focus is on a small number of cues
  - ✓ Broadening—focus must be on several different cues
- Direction of attention—either the focus is internal or external (cannot be both):
  - ✓ Internal—focus is directed inward toward thoughts and feelings
  - ✓ External—focus is directed outward into the environment, on defensive coverages or opponent rotations, for example

Concentration Training

To be effective at "freeing the mind," players must be able to foster adequate attention and concentration control. In other words, players must have the ability to focus and switch attention as needed during pressure situations. The following strategies can assist players in executing automatically and effectively.

This process begins by evaluating attentional strengths and weaknesses via the Offensive and Defensive Mental Skills Questionnaire in Chapter 4. Identify the important components of attention, including width (narrow or broad), direction (internal or external), and attentional switching.

Next, coaches can identify the attentional demands of volleyball and of specific positions (Figure 12-13) (Schmidt, Peper, & Wilson, 2001). Helping players realize the attentional demands of certain situations can assist them in focusing on the most relevant cues in an organized fashion. Those coaches who attend to the minute details of the game most likely teach their players these important attentional cues. Once players are armed with this information, they can simply focus on these relevant cues prior to execution, thus eliminating the distracting and harmful negative thoughts and self-talk and freeing themselves to play automatically.

The next section, "Physical/Mental Preparation and Readiness," describes how these attentional components can be organized prior to playing as pre-game routines or during play as execution routines.

Moreover, assessing the most common concentration problems in volleyball is another good strategy that coaches can utilize while teaching specific technical points (Figures 12-13 and 12-14) (Nideffer, 1976; Ziegler, 2002). For players to be in control of their thoughts and emotions before each ball contact, it is important that they are aware of their thoughts and feelings, as well as the specific cues they should be attending to and the ones they should eliminate. Having an attentional focus that is too narrow-internal, for example, at the wrong time could confuse the player due to focusing on inappropriate cues (internal distractions), rather than cues in the environment (e.g., location of opposing hitters, number of blockers at the net).

	Attentional Demands			
	Broad		Narrow	
Sport Situation	Internal	External	Internal	External
Ex. 1: a libero positioning on a high set to the outside	How did I cover it last time?	Location of set in relation to net and our block	Focus on getting hands to ball	Pass nails!
Ex. 2: serving	Serve to area 3 with speed	Where is the weak passer?	Pre-serve routine	Smooth swing

Figure 12-13. Attentional demands of positional play

Attentional Style	**Benefits to Using**	**Cost to Using** Mistakes due to ......
Broad external	good awareness of sport environment	...attending to distracting cues (Ex.: bad call from ref; crowd noise)
Broad internal	good planning-strategic thinking	...overanalysis = thinking too much (Ex.: hesitation; apprehension)
Narrow external	can effectively lock in on a couple of cues	...too narrow = miss critical cues (Ex.: too focused on player or ball)
Narrow internal	good at locking in on a single thought	...could *choke* = too internal (Ex.: too much in head = negativity)

Figure 12-14. Cost-benefit of attentional styles

Be aware of other variables that can impact a player's ability to control his attentional capacity. It is important to realize the relationship between intensity and attention. Players who become overly tense and anxious will have a difficult time keeping their focus on the important cues. Some will keep switching from internal to external stimuli, which will lead to overload and confusion. The athlete could lose confidence, which will further increase anxiety and tension, and worsen performance. Some players, when facing adversity and increased pressure or anxiety, will fall back on their most preferred attentional style, which may be wrong for the particular situation. Anxiety and tension can also cause difficulties in properly switching from one attentional style to another (direction and width).

Internal and external distractions are also of concern. Figure 12-15 lists pertinent sources of distractions, both internal and external (Voight, 2000b).

Internal Distractions	External Distractions
• focus on irrelevant performance cues • inability to switch attention from one play to another • focus on past mistakes or future concerns • worry over outcome • fear of failure • inability to "quiet the mind"; being too much "in the head" • negative self-talk • worry over expectations of others • indecision during play (lack of trust/confidence) • "what if" statements • uncertainty • selfish thinking	• media coverage • interviews with media • presence of family and friends • presence of a mass of fans who may have traveled from afar • spectator distractions during play • visual distractions • auditory distractions • verbal abuse • pressure from boosters, administrators to win (benefits to school) • seeding/ranking • playing a "giant killer" • playing on the road • playing at home • previous performance against opponent

Figure 12-15. Internal and external distractions

One of the major ways distractions affect performance is by consuming limited attentional capacities. Instead of using attentional resources to focus on the necessary performance cues—physical, technical, strategic, or mental—players wastefully attend to distractions, which either do nothing to aid performance or actually cause performances to suffer. Attending to distractions also evokes *psychological* reactions such as negative, deprecating thoughts, worry, or uncertainty; *physiological* reactions such as tense muscles, shallow breathing, or rigid movements; or *emotional* reactions like anger, frustration, or a loss of control. Conversely, these responses can take many athletes off their game. They not only waste time and effort, but these responses can definitely have an adverse effect on preparation and performance.

Figure 12-16. The crowd could be a major distraction for some players.

A third way in which distractions affect performance is through the narrowing of attentional focus, which causes *choking*. When players get too negative, worried, or anxious, their focus narrows as they attend to less of what they should be focusing on. This causes critical cues to be blocked out that are necessary for effective execution. Blocking out the cues can cause some players to miss easy kills, lead to poor passing, or cause players to get caught watching the wrong cues—and hundreds of other dysfunctional plays.

As shown in Figures 12-12, 12-13, and 12-14, each attentional dimension is valuable, as long as players engage the right dimension for the right situation. The next section of this chapter delves into greater detail of how to incorporate these attentional dimensions into preparatory and execution routines. Utilizing preparatory and execution routines to better organize the time prior to the serve can incorporate numerous mental skill–training strategies already discussed.

Physical/Mental Preparation and Readiness

One of the most important factors contributing to top performance is the ability to generate and maintain optimal readiness prior to competition. At the elite level, where athletes possess similar sport-specific and physical abilities, the way athletes engage their thoughts and emotions before a competition could be the difference between winning and losing. Two methods used to improve physical, mental, and emotional readiness are the use of *pre-performance* and *execution routines*. Pre-performance and execution routines typically consist of thought components like concentration, productive thoughts, and self-talk; behavioral elements such as walk-throughs and individual rituals; and finally, energizing components like ensuring adequate rest, energy, and hydration. This section outlines ways to help players establish comprehensive, yet simple to apply, pre-serve and pre-game routines that will both encapsulate tough thinking and feeling and appropriate attentional dynamics.

Figure 12-12, used earlier to detail attentional components, also represents the stages of a pre-serve or execution routine. These four types of attentional focus can be part of a preparatory routine for setters, outsides, opposites, middles, and defensive specialists. The following example of a pre-serve routine is designed for setters. First, once the setter gets into position for the next serve, his attention should be on assessing the situation *(broad external focus)* in terms of defensive coverage and

Courtesy of SCVC & Ralf's Photography

Figure 12-17. Setters must be able to switch their attentional focus to be most effective.

rotation. Second, the setter must analyze the play to be run *(broad internal focus)* and what his primary responsibility is on the play, while also communicating the play to the team. Third, the setter must prepare himself for the serve *(narrow internal focus)*, giving special attention to focus in on one or two specific cues (thus blocking out distractions and negative thoughts). Once the setter gets into position, he should then be operating on automatic processing *(narrow external focus)*, letting all of his practice, preparation, talent, and skill take over. Thinking is replaced by automatically reacting to what the scene and situation dictate.

A preparatory routine such as this not only helps mentally and emotionally prepare players for the next play, but it also can be quite beneficial in helping let go of mistakes such as passing errors, mental mistakes, or misreading coverages. This will enable them to play in the present and take one play at a time. Instead of focusing on past mistakes (thinking in the past), players are instructed to focus on the steps of the routine. *Refocusing* routines can also be used to help deal with frustration, worries, negative thoughts, and self-talk during play. By focusing "in" on this routine, players will be blocking "out" potential distractions.

Preparation and readiness for games should begin well before stepping onto the game court. Having an organized pre-game routine can greatly improve a player's ability to free his head by focusing in on critical elements that help him prepare and get ready for the game. These routines can also guard against distractions, pre-game anxieties, and a loss in focus. To truly achieve optimal readiness, athletes must focus their attention on what their specific needs are prior to playing. If these are not inherently apparent, have players brainstorm the specifics behind their best and worst performances (Figure 12-18).

	Best performance	Worst performance
physically feel =		
emotionally feel =		
what you were thinking =		
what your behaviors were =		
how was your self-talk? what you were saying to yourself =		
how did you deal with distractions? what the distractions were =		

Figure 12-18. Brainstorming pre-game needs

Upon completion of the "brainstorming" chart, determine the differences between the best and worst performances and prioritize what really helped versus what really hurt preparation and performance. Have players insert them into the chart in Figure 12-19.

What Really *Helped* You?	What Really *Hurt* Your Game?
*	*
*	*
*	*
*	*
*	*
*	*

Figure 12-19. Prioritizing pre-game routine components

Players should then use the listed information to come up with their ideal pre-game routine, including: What physical feelings are needed? What emotional needs must be met? What thoughts are preferred? What behaviors are conducive? What should the self-talk include? And finally, what is the best way to keep focus? Devising the pre-game routine then entails prioritizing specific elements based upon the timing leading up to the big event:

- 48 hours prior to game time
- 24 hours prior to game time
- Morning of the game
- 2 hours before game time
- 1 hour before game time
- Just prior to the first serve

During the flow of play, when a player finds himself struggling with making plays, he should be able to rely on pre-set *coping routines* to help him get back on his game. These coping routines can be executed just prior to the preparatory routine, especially if he is in need to letting go of a past mistake. Some examples of specific elements that can be included in a coping routine include the following:

- A subtle way of letting go of any pent-up frustration over a past mistake, such as clenching the fist, then releasing the tension; clapping hands; pounding fist to hand, or verbally letting it out without making a spectacle

- Routines that can include pre-selected phrases such as "I'm ready", "forget the mistake," or "focus on your role," to help focus on the next play while leaving the past play in the past
- Triggers or actions that symbolically "wipe" away the past mistake or distraction; for example, wiping hands so as to wipe the mistake away
- Performance cues as reminders of what needs to be done right now to succeed; for example, one or two tactical points like "OK, let's take care of the ball better on this possession," "quickly scan the opponents' positioning," or "quick steps, early platform"
- Deep breaths along with some motivating self-talk to get back into form; focusing on the strengths of your game, as well as intently focusing on what needs to be done with the next serve of the ball will help to block out distractions while helping players perform past their potential

Some teams go a bit further and devise *team coping routines* so when they are having a rough time and momentum is working against them, they are able to stay connected and begin making plays again. Components of the team routine can include ensuring that the team stays vocal, always come together for a "five," and use their teammates' "buttons." These "buttons" refer to what each teammate needs from their teammates when things are not going their way. For example, some players want their teammates to give them "fives," others want words of encouragement, while others want to be challenged to get the job done. When teammates are armed with this information, they can step in and say/do the right thing to help their teammate get back into the game.

Inspirational Toughness

The last barrier to address is a lack of *inspirational* toughness. This component has to do with why an athlete plays the sport and what makes athletes the happiest while playing. Athletes play sports for hundreds of reasons—do you know why your players play volleyball? What is each getting out of the experience? Very often players' motives for playing are incongruent with their coaches' motives.

Some coaches believe that all players play to get better and move along to the next level, but unless players are asked what their motives are and have some of their motives met they will not be optimally motivated and inspired. Athletes are driven by these motives. Some players play just to be affiliated with a team, others play for the recognition and accolades, and others play for the camaraderie of teammates. Athletes who are not having their primary motives met are less driven to work toward the coach's motives, such as better play, wins, or championships, and are thus limited by this inspirational barrier.

Asking players what their primary motives are for playing, as well as what their future aspirations in volleyball are, will truly help coaches gain access to their players' inner drives and motivations. Players who are not aware of these primary motives are unable to maximize their playing capacities because inspiration is what drives players to get better in all aspects of their games.

Sacrifice, work ethic, commitment, dedication, risk taking, and drive are all words that define the inner core of competitiveness. This inner core is what inspires a player and team to do what they do.

Chapter Summary

- Those athletes who are more aware of their thoughts and self-talk and also develop plans for dealing with inappropriate and damaging thoughts and self-talk, are more consistent performers and perform better in pressure situations.
- When most players think about negative things and get down on themselves, they usually play their worst volleyball.
- Confident athletes believe that every time out on the court, that can and will play well. Players who are able to think this way do not let their play dictate their confidence. Rather, their confidence level remains high, thus dictating their performance.
- Taking advantage of the many sources of performance confidence can be a tremendous way to optimize player confidence and performance.
- Gaining control and mastery over intensity is one of the most important things players (and coaches) can do to improve practice and game readiness.
- Being overintense is not the only way that intensity can impede players' progress. Being underintense has its own causes and performance consequences.

- To be effective at "freeing the mind," players must be able to foster adequate attention and concentration control. This means having the ability to focus and switch attention as needed during pressure situations.
- One of the major ways distractions affect performance is by consuming limited attentional capacities. Attending to these distractions evokes psychological, physiological, or emotional reactions that can take many players off their top games.
- One of the more important factors contributing to top performances is the ability to generate and maintain optimal readiness prior to execution.

Section IV:
Training and Coaching
Effectiveness

13

Quality of Practice: Coach and Player Responsibilities

Although automaticity may come a little easier and quicker to those who have loads of natural talent, all players need to work to improve upon their skills and mechanics by putting in their reps. A universal goal for coaches of all sports is to maximize the efficiency of practice time. Practice is where it all gets done—the physical training, the technical work, the implementation of systems, the training of their mental games, and the simulation of game conditions so players are totally prepared for match play.

The quality of an individual athlete's practices is considered one of the most critical determinants of optimal performance. Unfortunately for coaches and athletes, there has been a paucity of material available that addresses how to maximize practice opportunities. Thus, the purpose of this section is to address this topic from an integrated approach that links the responsibilities of both players and coaches to improve upon the quality of individual and team training.

Utilizing the theoretical, empirical, and practical work from numerous disciplines (e.g., motor learning, pedagogy, and applied sport psychology), four major factors have been developed that encapsulate the most important areas that both athletes and coaches should address to improve the quality of training of the individual and team—attitude, preparation, execution and evaluation. These four main factors will be discussed in detail, ranging from coach and player attitudes toward training and specific preparation practices, to *execution* strategies and finally *evaluating* one's performance after training.

Quality of Training—Athletes' Responsibilities

Quality Attitude

For athletes to train to the upper range of their potential, it is critical that they take responsibility from the onset for improving upon the quality of their training by adopting a quality attitude. Pete Carroll, head football coach at repeat national champion USC, spoke at a conference and stated that an important distinction exists between players who have a professional attitude versus those with a mediocre attitude. The major difference between these two attitudes is how players perceive practice. Some players view practice as an opportunity to play and improve, which denotes an internally driven motivation mainly within the player's control. Others, however, perceive practice as something that is "done to them," signifying an externally driven motivation that is out of a player's control (Voight, 2002).

If a player has a mediocre attitude, his effort in practice will fluctuate depending upon mood, whether or not he likes the activity, or on external motivation. Players with this mindset go through the motions, put in their time, and just want to complete the drill and get off the court. Players with a professional attitude, on the other hand, view practice as an opportunity for improvement and refinement, not something "forced" onto them. Such athletes ask these questions: How can I/we get better today? What are I/we going to accomplish today? Athletes set standards of performance for each practice/week of practice, and evaluate their practice performance in terms of execution, effort, and overall quality, while also seeking feedback regarding their practice performance.

"One of the things I believe strongly about is putting responsibility on your players: You want your players to be mature, to be accountable, and to understand that the success you are going to achieve is based upon their abilities, their commitment, and their motivation."
—Doug Beal, Head Coach, US Volleyball National Team
(*The Volleyball Coaching Bible*, 2002, p. 47)

Figure 13-1. Professional-attitude players view practice as an opportunity to improve technical execution.

Professional-attitude athletes take more responsibility for their performances by holding themselves accountable to pre-set standards of execution. Another important aspect of an athlete's attitude is their "coachability," which can be defined by the player's willingness to put in near-maximal effort on drill work and practice/competition, listen to coaching points and attempt to implement them into action, and accept feedback of all types (corrective, positive, punitive, encouragement). In most cases, a player's level of coachability can be altered, especially in the case of "uncoachable" players, although it takes work from all parties (coach, athletes, parents, friends, teammates) and a special coach to undo some of the wrongs that may have led to the present uncoachable condition.

Closely tied to coachability is the motivation and work rate of the players. Professional-attitude athletes tend to be motivated by internal desires to improve and perform better than their last performance, thus increasing their motivation and work rate to do all they can in practice to ensure this occurs. Conversely, mediocre-attitude athletes tend to be motivated by external agents (praise, big game, crowd, accolades, media), yet in the absence of these agents motivation is lacking, as is the case in practice settings. These mediocre-attitude athletes usually consider themselves "gamers" and do not feel it important to give a near-maximal effort in training. These players can also be considered as "part-time" players because they only really play at game-time. These "gamers" believe they can just turn on their top performances like a light without having to put in the work in practice. Although these players may be quite talented and succeed come game-time, their consistency of play will not be as sharp and their long-term progress may be jeopardized by the lack of consistent, quality practice.

Quality Preparation

How many players actually prepare for practice? Most probably shove down a burger, race to the locker room, busily put on their gear, get to the practice court and wait until they are told what to do. Sounds like a mediocre-attitude athlete. A professional-attitude athlete will attempt to find a way to prepare better for practice. Actually having a set routine to follow made up of proper eating (fueling up) and rest, as well as finding a way to let go of non-volleyball-related problems (school, friends, significant others), can ensure that the two hours of practice can be dedicated solely toward quality execution. The ability to park distractions is an important skill to acquire. It is very difficult to truly commit and focus on practice if outside stressors are brought into the gym. One routine that has worked with several top players is to write down the stressors that are nagging them and, prior to walking into the gym, shred or throw away this paper, symbolically throwing away the stressors so the player can focus on practice objectives.

> "Athletes ...know that a gap often exists between their knowledge and their behavior. There are those who usually do what is necessary; others often do what is necessary; some rarely do. Those who never do what is necessary are not around long enough to be otherwise convinced. Preparation is the key."
>
> —Harv Dorfman, Author, Mental-Skills Trainer for Major League Baseball (2003, p. 309)

Coaches can be a great help in assisting athletes with their practice preparation by setting up pre-practice routines, such as having players arrive to the court prior to the start of practice to perform a wide array of warm-ups activities. Players who do this can be truly ready to begin practice once the coaches arrive. Also, athletes can better prepare for practice by setting standards of performance (goals) for each week's practice or individual session (e.g., What do I want to accomplish by the first pre-season scrimmage? What do I want to accomplish in this blocking drill?). In addition to setting standards, players can *visualize* what they want to accomplish prior to physically and technically executing the drill. Another strategy that top players have used is to mentally picture themselves executing their most important shots over and over again, often the night before practice or prior to practice. Setters might set 100 sets a night before bedtime, or 50 sets before practice in their mind's eye. Hitters would hit line and angle, through the block, and around the block, over and over in their head. Each position could easily do this type of "homework" every day or night. Visualizing these swings helps to devise a mental blueprint that is used during real, physical training. The more players swing, both in their heads and with a real ball, the more reps they are putting in.

Quality Execution

Mediocre-attitude athletes often go through the motions and do just enough during practice so they do not get yelled at or called out. Professional-attitude athletes have set purposes and objectives for each practice session and view practice as a valuable practice opportunity. They also utilize techniques geared toward their own quality execution, whereas the "mediocres" basically attempt to survive the session.

Examples of quality execution techniques used by professional-attitude athletes include:
- Taking notes during a team meeting or after practice sessions regarding specific points they find important, especially coaching points on technical and tactical elements.
- Evaluating practice performance "on the fly" or during practice, so they can be better aware of what is working versus what is not. "Mediocres" just want to get to the end of practice and are not aware of how they are doing.
- Devising competitions with themselves to increase the quality of execution. For example, if a professional-attitude athlete is doing sprint work, he attempts to chase down a teammate and not just try to survive the running. During technical work, a professional-attitude athlete counts the number of successful attempts made instead of just doing the drill until the coach stops it (again, merely surviving).
- Utilizing preset routines can help when a player's concentration begins to drift during practice. Professional-attitude athletes utilize refocusing routines to ensure that when focus fades they have a routine from which to draw.
- Knowing exactly why they are doing a certain drill, what the end result should look like, and what they should be focusing on during execution can have a big impact on the quality of effort and execution. These issues should be discussed prior to drill execution. Although this responsibility primarily lies with the coaches, players should ask if they know the answer to these pertinent questions.
- A final recommendation is to not just let practice end—make sure that players finish practice.

Figure 13-2. Those players who consistently practice with quality effort and execution do so because they consciously decide to do so and use proven strategies to help them improve every day.

Quality Control

Once practice is done, do players evaluate their performances? Professional-attitude players ask themselves questions such as:

- How were my physical, technical, and tactical execution?
- How was my work rate?
- What were the strengths and weaknesses of my play?
- What will I do differently during my next practice?
- What should I do in preparation for next practice?
- What helped to motivate me for practice today?

- How did I refocus and stay focused today?
- What did the coaches say to me regarding my practice performance?

Mediocre-attitude players do not ask these questions—they are simply pleased that practice is over.

Using standards and goals is very helpful, especially if a coach has players evaluate their progress. If players accomplish a particular goal, they should take pride in their accomplishment and press on with higher goals. If goals are not accomplished, players should then reevaluate their performance (positives/negatives), and either start fresh to accomplish the goal tomorrow or revise the goal.

A survey has been developed to assess the use of the essential quality practice techniques by top players in their respective sports (Figure 13-4). Obtaining this feedback can be an excellent springboard for discussion with individual players and the team. Players should be informed of the results with the trust that they will only be used to assist them in their play, and not be used as a punishment in any way. For example, no player should be called out for having low scores on the subscales. Players will derive the appropriate feedback if they score it themselves as well, but this exercise will be more valuable if the coach is active in the process. As with any questionnaire, players can record answers that they know the coach wants to see, but this can be limited if the coach explains the importance of honest responses, and that the results will only be used to better the player's training habits.

Quality of Training—Coaches' Responsibilities

Quality Attitude

Coaches should do all they can to be aware of their specific coaching philosophy and behaviors, as well as the effects these attitudes and behaviors have on their athletes. As the leadership literature indicates, athletes have numerous preferences for specific coaching behaviors. If athletes feel they are not getting the adequate amount of a preferred coaching behavior, their level of satisfaction and performance could be hindered. The effect of this discrepancy between preferred and perceived behaviors could be further exacerbated by a lack of awareness on the part of the coach. Coaches who are more aware of their own attitudes and behaviors, and how their players perceive these, may have players who are more satisfied and perform better. It has been written that the quality of an athlete's sport experience reflects the beliefs and attitudes of the coach.

Another critical aspect of a coach's attitude is his openness to the mental aspects of sport. Although many coaches cite mental factors for the team's and players'

Figure 13-3. To be most effective, coaches must be aware of how their feedback and actions are perceived by their players—miscommunication leads to many barriers to optimal performance.

successes and failures, how many of these coaches actually train the mental side of their sport? As mentioned in Chapter 11, it is important for coaches to know that incorporating mental skills training into everyday coaching can enhance coaching effectiveness as well as players' quality of practice play, both of which can transfer onto the game court.

Many coaches, however, do put a priority on improving upon all aspects of their players' performance, especially the mental side. For example, some coaches help establish set routines whereby the players begin to prepare for practice before the opening whistle. Bruce Snyder, former head football coach at Arizona State University,

Training Survey

Please read each statement and fill in the most appropriate word by circling the corresponding number from 0 to 5 (never to always). *Note*: Your responses should refer to your usual training habits.

		KEY:			
Never: 0	*Rarely: 1*	*Sometimes: 2*	*Often: 3*	*Very often: 4*	*Always: 5*

1.)	I _____ look forward to practice.	0	1	2	3	4	5
2.)	I _____ "go through the motions" in practices.	0	1	2	3	4	5
3.)	I _____ consider practice to be an opportunity to improve.	0	1	2	3	4	5
4.)	Before practice, I _____ have in mind what I am going to try to improve.	0	1	2	3	4	5
5.)	I _____ feel that practice is something that coach "does to us."	0	1	2	3	4	5
6.)	I _____ look forward to the end of practice.	0	1	2	3	4	5
7.)	I _____ start thinking about practice well before it starts.	0	1	2	3	4	5
8.)	If I feel tired or do not like the drills, I _____ have a good practice.	0	1	2	3	4	5
9.)	I _____ use a routine to help get me "ready" for practice.	0	1		3	4	5
10.)	I _____ fuel up prior to practice by eating the right food and hydrating myself.	0	1	2	3	4	5
11.)	I _____ find out from the coaching staff what type of things we will do in practice for the week/upcoming session.	0	1	2	3	4	5
12.)	If available, I _____ review video tape of practices/ games to target my goals for practices.	0	1	2	3	4	5
13.)	I _____ ask for coaches' feedback to help target my practice goals.	0	1	2	3	4	5
14.)	I _____ do mental and physical preparation prior to practice.	0	1	2	3	4	5
15.)	I am _____ able to leave non-sport issues (classwork, family) and distractions outside of the practice gym.	0	1	2	3	4	5
16.)	I _____ do relaxation or "psych-up" techniques prior to practice if I feel I need it to get ready & motivated.	0	1	2	3	4	5
17.)	I _____ take notes during team meetings and video sessions.	0	1	2	3	4	5
18.)	During practice, I _____ evaluate my play in terms of what is working, what isn't, and areas I can improve.	0	1	2	3	4	5
19.)	I _____ put in maximal effort when I practice.	0	1	2	3	4	5
20.)	I _____ use a refocusing routine when I find myself "drifting" during practice.	0	1	2	3	4	5
21.)	During conditioning/fitness work, I _____ challenge myself by passing a teammate, or beating my last time.	0	1	2	3	4	5
22.)	I _____ try and help my teammates improve their work rate in practice via vocal encouragement and by my example.	0	1	2	3	4	5

Figure 13-4. Quality-of-training survey for players

23.) During drill work, I _____ use "challenging Games," like counting the number of successful reps, to improve my practice performance.	0	1	2	3	4	5
24.) I am _____ receptive to feedback regarding my play from teammates and coaches.	0	1	2	3	4	5
25.) After practice, I _____ evaluate what I did well, in addition to what I did not do well.	0	1	2	3	4	5
26.) After practice, I _____ ask my coaches for feedback regarding my practice performance.	0	1	2	3	4	5
27.) I _____ think about practice once it is over.	0	1	2	3	4	5
28.) After practice I _____ plan what I will work on for the next training session.	0	1	2	3	4	5
29.) If I feel I need added work in a particular part of my play, I will _____ spend extra time on it after practice.	0	1	2	3	4	5
30.) I _____ evaluate my mental game (strengths and weaknesses) upon completion of practice.	0	1	2	3	4	5
31.) I _____ think about how I can improve the mental aspects of my play.	0	1	2	3	4	5
32.) After practice, I _____ provide feedback to the coaches regarding the practice session (what I liked, what worked, what we need to do more of next time).	0	1	2	3	4	5

Scoring Procedures:
✓ High scores represent excellent training attitudes and habits
✓ Reverse score items 2, 5, and 6 (0=5; 1=4; 2=3; 3=2; 4=1; 5=0)
✓ Four Subscales: Scores range from 0–40
> Subscale 1: Questions 1–8 = Quality Attitude
> Subscale 2: Questions 9–16 = Quality Preparation
> Subscale 3: Questions 17–24 = Quality Execution
> Subscale 4: Questions 25–32 = Quality Control

✓ Subscale score ranges:
> *33–40   Wish the team were full of these "trainers"! You are fully maximizing your capacities.
> *25–32   Very good training habits! Always do what is necessary.
> *17–24   Good training habits overall—some areas are in need of attention; often do what is necessary.
> *9–16   Poor training habits—some real work is necessary to improve; rarely do what is necessary.
> *0–8   Bad training habits—will catch up with you someday; never do what is necessary.

✓Quality Attitude =   _____
✓Quality Preparation =   _____
✓Quality Execution =   _____
✓Quality Control =   _____

did just this by creating a set of routines designed so players could leave their school, family, friends, and other college issues/concerns in their cars or their rooms (referred to as "parking"), and not take them into the locker room. Thus, once they entered the locker room they were football players, and their entire focus was on this endeavor.

Quality Preparation

The first strategy that can be used to enhance preparation is helping players devise individual standards and goals for the upcoming practices. Players who are informed about the objectives, the standards to which they will be held, and the ways in which they can meet the standards and accomplish the goals, will have a more motivated, productive attitude. Thus, these athletes may be better prepared for the practice session than those players who go into practice uninformed. Players who are uninformed and not given explicit directions and standards are more likely to simply go through the motions if left to their own devices. Additionally, using different modalities (e.g., teaching styles) to communicate these important messages, such as verbal communication, graphical displays, and physical demonstrations, has been shown to be effective pedagogical strategies.

A second method used to improve preparation is to teach players how to improve focus, as well as ways to reestablish focus when facing adversity. First, coaches can setup pre-practice routines for players with the goal of helping them park stressors and distractions outside of the gym. Some coaches have established a "concentration line," or a funnel that players must walk across/through prior to entering practice so players can focus on training rather than on all their non-volleyball issues and problems. Additionally, players who lose focus during practice should have preset refocusing routines handy. The University of Nebraska Football coaches, with the help of mental trainer Ken Ravizza (Osbourne & Ravizza, 1988), formulated a routine that helped to instill a sense of "refocus" once the players began to drift, thus causing a breakdown in play execution. This routine was called the three R's, *Ready-Respond-Refocus*. It was so useful that they began to use it during games when the quarterback needed his teammates to listen to the play call in the huddle. Other examples of preparation and execution routines are listed in Chapter 12. Through the use of standards and refocusing routines, players' preparation for practice may be greatly enhanced, thus improving upon quality execution.

Another important area for self-examination for coaches is a critique of the structure of practice sessions. According to the motor learning research literature, learning is enhanced if the practice environment is structured according to the following principles of practice: teaching progressions, practice variability, and game simulation.

Players who are being taught either new skills or new "wrinkles" to old skills, should be brought through deliberate skill progressions ranging from the simple to the complex. What makes the progressions complex is the variability of practice, which includes predesigned conditions that increase visual and auditory distractions so the skill is performed under changing conditions. These visual and auditory distractions, also referred to as contextual interference elements, can range from changing the speed and timing with which the particular skill pattern is executed, to performing the skill under the pressure of opposition or space or practicing specific game conditions (e.g., scrimmaging with the score set at 25-25, or being down or up late in the game). Coaches cannot expect their players to execute in pressure situations if they do not simulate these situations during practice time. Ken Ravizza, mental trainer for several professional teams, advises coaches to practice between-game talks and time-outs. This is done so players will practice listening and applying what was said on the game court during pressure situations. Thus, it is very important to simulate game conditions in practice sessions by increasing the use of contextual interference variables.

Coaches who are cognizant of the ways in which teaching progressions, practice variability, and contextual interference can affect players' practices are in better positions to continue to increase the learning and performing of their athletes. Taking the time needed to address these concerns while preparing for practice sessions seems warranted.

Quality Execution

As previously stated, simulating game situations in practice is critical for enhancing upon the players' execution during match play. Ensuring the players have been immersed in all that will occur during an actual game prepares them for what they will experience later, including the speed of play, potential distractions, and pressure situations. Anson Dorrance, head women's soccer coach at North Carolina (a dynasty in women's soccer), not only does this, but he and his staff also chart competitions between players. For example, they chart fitness tests, one-on-one duels, small team matches, and technical skill checks to enhance competitiveness by pitting teammate against teammate. His players have repeatedly stated that match play is actually easier than their practice sessions (Dorrance, 1996).

Another way to improve execution is the advantageous use of "teachable moments." Research has indicated that the appropriate use of feedback is a critical determinant to learning. Teachable moments are those prime opportunities coaches use to teach, instruct, direct, encourage, praise, and punish. Spotting these moments is one of the challenges, the other being what to do with these teachable moments. Being able to differentiate between very good, good, or poor technical execution takes time, experience, and expertise. When you catch players doing technical and tactical elements correctly, this is an ideal "teachable moment" because it acts as a model—a picture of how it should be done. Although corrective feedback is important, all players like to hear when they are doing something well. The challenge for them and their teammates is to repeat this positive, productive action.

The following strategies can help in analyzing skill execution (Fischman & Oxendine, 1998):

- Make several observations to compare players' patterns of execution with correct technique. Taking only a quick look can bias the needs analysis.
- Select one error at a time, identifying the most critical error first, specifying the particular part of the skill that went wrong.
- Determine the cause of the error and specify what the athlete must do to correct it. Keep in mind that hasty error correction may not lead to an increase in performance since it could cause the athlete to doubt the ability and knowledge of his coaches.
- Stop the action to offer praise and encouragement (catch players doing things right) if it is deserved. The critical word in the previous sentence is "deserved." If coaches go too far and offer too much praise, especially if the action was fundamental and not praiseworthy, the coach will lose credibility and the players will then perceive that a lower standard is now accepted.

In addition, feedback may be provided to motivate and energize, not just to provide critical performance information, such as error correction, knowledge of results and performance, specific teaching cues, reinforcement, and punishment. The less frequent the feedback, the more empowering the feedback becomes. Too much feedback may become distracting to the players, as well as cause them to think too much about their performance (paralysis by overanalysis). Finally, feedback should be provided during skill execution (concurrent) or at the conclusion of the skill pattern (terminal). A good mix of both is recommended.

Two notable coaches have commented on the importance of types and content of feedback with their elite players and teams. Tony Dicicco, former coach of the Women's World Cup Soccer championship team, has been noted as stressing the importance of these teachable moments by catching players doing things right and not always waiting for a mistake to occur to offer feedback. Pete Carroll, head football coach at USC, noted that timing and content of feedback are critical to improving subsequent performance. He believes that the sooner the correction the better, and if the players are corrected negatively, they will only remember the negative. Therefore, if the corrective feedback is consistently negative, the real message is not getting across to the athletes and subsequent learning and change will seldom occur, thereby wasting the teachable moment. Providing negative messages not only confuses players, but it also serves to de-motivate and un-inspire. If coaches have to yell at players during matches, then they have not properly taught the players during practice all week. Harvey Dorfman has detailed the importance of using "real language," or, as he stated, "mapping out the real territory in real language" (2003, p. 50).

- Be specific, not vague
- Know the difference between verifiable feedback and feedback that is based on opinion and judgments
- When comparisons are used, ensure that they are accurate and to the point
- Be concise when instructing—players want to play and not sit and listen to speeches
- Watch the use of "emotional" words, such as "he's a wimp"
- Avoid generalizations—to make a point stick the coach needs to be able to verify what he says
- Make distinctions "between fact (the final score), inference (we lost because you didn't come to play), and value judgment (the officials were out to get us)"

> *"If you yell at them after every mistake, you will stifle their growth. They will become tentative when they need to be aggressive, and their minds will get in the way of their progress."*
> —Pete Waite, Head Volleyball Coach, Wisconsin
> (*The Volleyball Coaching Bible*, 2002, p. 304)

Other methods of improving team execution are creative scoring methods and alternating starters and reserve players during game scrimmages. First, through the use of creative scoring methods, coaches can emphasize what they want players to work on within game-simulated drills and scrimmages. The teams may continue to play from the score of 27-27 to work on their "finishing" ability, or begin by having the starting team, side "A," down by two, or up by two on side "B" (reserves). These scenarios are often switched to see which team can battle through to find ways of winning. Mick Haley, head women's volleyball coach at USC, often takes his better players and has them play on side B, and also has back-up players play on side A. He borrowed this concept from head football coach Pete Carroll. "One thing Pete does is take the starting quarterback and give him a bunch of reps with the B squad, which helps liven that squad up. The B offense works a lot harder because they know they have the starter taking snaps behind them. And the quarterback knows he has to step up his play to win with that particular squad" (Anderson, 2003, p. 21). Coach Haley states that moves such as these increase the capabilities of both sides, thus improving the overall team.

A final point to improving the quality of execution is to utilize different teaching modalities so as to appeal to every athlete's most salient learning style. Such styles include visual (e.g., walk-throughs, shadow training, use of video, and chalk-talks), auditory (e.g., verbal instruction, lectures), kinesthetic (e.g., focus on how the action or movement feels), and imagery (e.g., visualize the tactical strategy or technique prior to actually acting it out). Utilize different teaching modalities and provide for adequate repetition of the desired technical skills to bring about optimal learning and transfer of skill from one drill to the next. Continuous repetitions, referred to as overlearning, is an important contributor to optimal learning and should be practiced especially with beginning skill learners, but even with those elite athletes who have made modifications to an already well-learned motor program (e.g., changing a hitter's approach).

Figure 13-5. Effective coaches use different modalities to reach and teach each one of their players.

Quality Control

Quality control refers to methods coaches can utilize to determine the effectiveness of their coaching behaviors, practice sessions, and ways they have attempted to assist their athletes in preparing and executing better in practice. Some methods are available that coaches can utilize to evaluate the effectiveness of the players in accomplishing the objectives of the training sessions. Charting, as described earlier, may aid in motivation and accountability, and increase the quality of subsequent training sessions. Giving fitness tests before and during the season, formally and informally testing tactical and strategic awareness (plays, game strategy, assignments), and grading positional assignments in terms of execution and corrections will all help in evaluating practice quality.

Maintaining open lines of communication between players and coaches is another key determinant of optimal coach, player, and team effectiveness. Coaches who have players who feel comfortable talking with them about their feelings and perceptions (how things are going) will gain a better understanding of not only their athletes and team but a greater awareness of how their own attitudes and coaching behaviors are affecting their players. Coaches can set up formal and informal meetings on a regular basis with their players to evaluate not only player progress but the coaching staff's progress regarding quality practice.

Coaches should also evaluate whether the amount of practice was beneficial in terms of positive training stress. If players begin to get overtrained (training stress exceeds athletes' capabilities to recover adequately), not only will their performance suffer but they also may experience emotional, psychological, and physiological consequences. (Voight, 2003). See Chapter 8 for more information on the deleterious effects of excessive training stress and under recovery on physical and mental well-being. Careful and smart implementation of overload and training stress should be evaluated by coaches after each training session. In addition to evaluating training stress, Schmidt and Wrisberg (2000) recommend using a checklist to evaluate your instructional strategies in terms of practice preparation (e.g., goal setting and identifying target skills), practice structure, presentation (e.g., clarifying expectations), and feedback.

Finally, coaches should also evaluate themselves and their staff on the amount of effort invested into the preparation and execution of practice sessions. As Anson Dorrance wrote, "Some coaches are no longer willing to make the emotional commitment needed to motivate players to attain the standard required of them to compete successfully at the highest level" (1996, p. 21). Due to this lack of emotional commitment, Dorrance reported that some coaches will not confront players who are not exerting maximal effort and thus end up having practice sessions that are easy and fun to run but do little to maximize learning and performance.

Chapter Summary

- A universal goal for coaches of all sports is to maximize the efficiency of practice time.
- Four major factors encapsulate the most important areas that both players and coaches should address to improve the quality of training. These areas are: adopting a quality attitude, utilizing quality preparation techniques, practicing quality execution strategies, and taking the time after practice for a quality evaluation.
- The quality of individual and team practice performance relies on an interactive process between players and coaches. Both parties have certain responsibilities that they must contribute for quality training to result.
- Some players view practice as an opportunity to play and improve, which denotes internally driven motivation, while others perceive practice as being externally driven and something that is "done to them."
- Together, the quality of team and individual training can improve, thus elevating the team and individual players' potential for quality play at game-time.
- It is very important that coaches do all they can to create an atmosphere that fosters quality attitude, quality preparation, quality execution, and quality control.

14

Quality Coaching: Beyond the X's and O's

Coaching "beyond the X's and O's" requires some additional time to adequately apply some of the important concepts and strategies contained within this book. Devoting time to strengthen your players' mental toughness skills will be well worth it because helping players in automating their execution will greatly improve play, both on an individual and team level. The most important concepts and techniques for coaches to address with their players and team include: helping players' improve their awareness of their technical and mental mechanics; the importance of automating their execution; the many performance barriers standing in the way of automatic execution; how these barriers specifically affect mechanical, mental, and performance proficiency via information processing and sequencing errors; and finally, toughness training exercises used to not only combat performance barriers but to overcome the debilitating effects of mechanical breakdowns. Adding these technical and mental mechanics to players' arsenals will not only better prepare them for game-time, but also help them consistently execute on the practice court day in and day out.

This final chapter asks you, the coach, to go a little further with your mental game by applying coaching effectiveness practices. For youth coaches especially, this chapter details "developmental coaching" methods to assist youth players in their physical, technical, mental, and social development. For competitive-level coaches, this chapter details the qualities and practices of effective sport leaders taken from research on coaching effectiveness and anecdotal reports from the coaches and athletes themselves.

Youth Coaching Effectiveness

"The mentality in youth sport needs to change. How can coaches teach valuable lessons about preparing youth for life when their value is based only on wins and losses?"

—Steve Courson, former NFL player
(*Los Angeles Times*, April 28, 2005)

When coaches agree to coach youth players there is a lot of responsibility bestowed on these club or youth coaches. These coaches are responsible for the physical safety of their players, as well as for their social and psychological welfare via an educational and fun sport experience. Because some coaches are working with younger players, they are also responsible for helping them improve their basic movement patterns (see Chapter 1 for examples), as well as teaching the fundamental technical skills of volleyball. Coaches who only value the outcome will be doing their players a great disservice by not teaching them important fundamental movement and technical skills. The consequences of this type of coaching could include injury, because players may be pushed too hard physically by attempting to play the game like their collegiate or professional idols before they have the requisite skill set. Psychologically, this type of coaching for youth players adversely affects their perceptions of competence, satisfaction, motivation, and willingness to continue playing the sport (even if the team wins).

There are many age-specific, developmental concerns that coaches should be made aware of, especially those who coach players who are 16 years and younger. It has been reported in the developmental research that the quality and extent of a child's activity influence his motor and intellectual development. Although children's motor ability is partially determined by heredity, other factors combine to improve a child's potential, including activity level, environmental factors (e.g., nutrition, illness, rest), social (e.g., level of sport, support from family and coaches), psychological (e.g., stress, lack of self-confidence, coping ability, experience), and physical development (e.g., growth rates).

Although children proceed through predictable patterns of motor and intellectual development, they develop proficiency at different rates. Coaches and parents alike should be cautioned about "pushing" their children/players to perform skills and activities before they are maturationally ready (physically, intellectually, socially). What could occur as a result includes accidents and physical injury, as well as long-term effects, such as instilling attitudes of fear, failure, low self-esteem, and low motivation to continue playing. Maureen Weiss, a renowned youth sport researcher, wrote that coaches and parents should be aware that physical skill alone is not sufficient enough in considering a child's skill expectations and their potential in the sport.

Based upon the human development, developmental psychology, motor development, motor learning, and the pedagogy fields, the following considerations address specific developmental and age-related differences that coaches should be familiar with if working with the youth sport athlete. Figure 14-1 details the most important concerns and how coaches can best address these developmental needs, and thus become more responsible and more effective coaches and educators.

According to this research, younger athletes should not be rushed developmentally or technically. Much like you would not want to teach a seven year old a split-fingered fastball (in baseball), you do not want players swinging with wanton abandon or diving for loose balls all over the gym. If players are not physically, mentally, or technically ready for such skills, forcing them to perform them will have a deleterious effect on the player in so many areas. Players who are eight and younger also do not need to listen to a coach talk and talk. These young players are kinesthetically inclined and learn by doing, not by watching or listening. Coaches who get too caught up in hearing themselves talk will only lose their players interest and force them to entertain themselves, which usually equates to messing around with a teammate. This "misbehaving" then upsets the coach due to them not being good listeners. It is not the players' fault in this case—let them play coach!

What coaches say and how they treat individual players becomes critical for eight- and nine-year-old players. Coaches who favor certain players, whether the coach realizes he is doing it or not, will be "caught" in the act by these perceptive youngsters. Coaches must be careful to play and treat everyone equally. At this age level, everyone should play the same amount of time and the atmosphere should be one of having fun and playing as a collective unit. Feedback and attention from coaches is cherished by players of this age, so do not hold back on providing positive words, especially if it is deserved. This feedback becomes even more important because players use this feedback to assist in developing their own sense of competence. The greater the feelings of competence, the more motivated players become, leading them to continue to try new skills and play as hard as they can. The primary focus must be on developing a fun team climate, followed by the acquisition of fundamental physical and technical skills. Game outcome should not even be brought up in conversation. Thus, team most valuable player awards, tournament trophies, and other outcome-related awards should be kept in the stores until these players rise through the competitive levels.

Coaching 10 to 12 year olds can be the "best and the worst" of times. Coaches must realize that developmentally these players are changing, almost right in front of them. Coaching the process of improving as a player should be paramount. Since most of these players' motor skills are well developed and automatic by this age, skill development should be a priority, especially with proper execution and functionality of

	Developmental Concerns	**Coach Applications**
Middle Childhood (ages 6-12)		
6-8 years old:	• importance of basic motor patterns (hand-eye coordination, footwork, balance, jumping) • up to 8 years old, all learn kinesthetically rather than auditorily or visually	• important not to rush young athletes along—just getting the basic movement patterns is critical • less *talking*, more *doing*—players learn by physical trial-and-error
8-9 years old:	• prefer the use of *adult* feedback to judge their own competencies • very much aware of individual differences (e.g., who's the best player and who's the worst) • importance of modeling of same-sex parent • very responsive to team/group activities	• need to hear confidence-enhancing feedback from coaches and parents • aware of players who get treated differently • look to parent(s) for modeling behaviors (comments made, overt behaviors before/during/after games)
10-12 years old:	• begin perfectionistic thinking (get discouraged easily when not perfect—especially those with low confidence) • will lose interest in activity if pressured • prefer to be given more responsibility • prefer to be talked to as an "equal" • respond well to caring, mature adults • rebellious and overcritical of self and others • motor skills learned during early years are now automatic • skill development now includes accuracy, coordination, and functionality of movements • preference for *adult* feedback wanes—increase in reliance on peer comparison and evaluation	• coach and parents need to be careful not to associate athletic performance to their child's/player's personality (having a bad game does not equate to being a bad person—it is only a game) • especially if a player has low self-confidence already, more pressure may drive him out of the game • must be taught that making mistakes and failing (losing) are part of the process of learning your game and becoming a better athlete • skill fundamentals are still critical—help make learning and practicing the FUNdamentals FUN • stress the importance of performing better than *you* did yesterday—deemphasize social comparison

Figure 14-1. Youth coaching effectiveness—developmental considerations

movement and decision-making. Players at this age base a lot of their perceptions of competence on how they stack up against their peers, or in the case of sports, against their opponents. Coaches and parents should stress the importance of playing better

	Developmental Concerns	Coach Applications
Adolescence (ages 12-17) 13-14 years old:	• period of *egocentrism* • personal uniqueness, "untouchable" • "imaginary audience"—believe they are center of attention, that people are either admiring or critical of them (in actuality, other adolescents are more concerned with being observed than with being the observer!) • continued preference for peer comparison and evaluation • emotional instability coupled with "know-it-all" mentality	• helpful for coaches to realize that teenagers do follow these particular "peculiarities," so they should not take it personally when players show these behaviors • "calling players out" to make a point (singling them out for doing something wrong) usually does not have the desired effects, especially long term—players are more concerned with being embarrassed than they are about learning a lesson
15-16 years old:	• begin to see themselves in "new light"; show empathy for others (volunteer activities), yet still display some egocentric thoughts and motives	• try to deemphasize comparing their performance with everyone else (uncontrollable and no-win game)—attempt to get players to use self-comparison (try to improve on what *you* did last time = internal criteria of success) • provide feedback that is commensurate with degree of skill/drill difficulty (if easy skill, don't praise)

Figure 14-1 (cont'd.) Youth coaching effectiveness—developmental considerations

than they did the last practice or game, as opposed to being the best player on the court. Coaches also must be careful to not associate performing on the court to player personality traits. For example, never tell a player that he is not mentally tough because he missed a serve on game point. Also, players begin to adopt perfectionistic reasoning, so players must be taught that mistakes are only part of the process of becoming a better player, and this message needs to be repeated as often as possible with players at this age level.

Courtesy of SCVC & Ralf Photography

Figure 14-2. Successful youth coaches apply developmental coaching to their players, which aids in development and enhances the sport experience.

Once players hit adolescence, between the ages of 12 and 17, they vacillate between emotional instability and a "know-it-all" attitude. Although they will listen to the coach (for the most part), their primary preference for feedback comes from their teammates and friends. Since adolescent players are so preoccupied with being "observed," penalizing players in front of their teammates is not an effective teaching tool. Players at this stage are engrossed in their own thinking and perceptions (egocentrism), so comparing them to other players or teams is not usually a viable form of motivation. It usually causes the players to become even more internal and self-conscious, and usually lowers player confidence while increasing anxiety and tension (emotional instability). Toward the end of this stage, players show empathy towards others and begin to look beyond their own personal "worlds," yet they are still quite sensitive about public criticism, so coaches should continue to provide negative feedback on a personal basis.

Competitive-Level Coaching Effectiveness

Process over Outcome

So many of today's schools, club organizations, and collegiate programs operate from the professional sport model, which is equated to a win-at-all-cost orientation. Steve Courson's quote cited earlier in this chapter mentioned the importance of coaches changing their "mentality." Youth coaches' becoming more aware of the developmental needs of their athletes and specifically addressing these concerns in their coaching is a step toward changing the current mentality. Another step that could be taken is for coaches to embrace the process rather than the outcome. At the collegiate level, the expectations can be so very high that it is difficult for coaches and players not to feel pressure about winning another tournament or national championship. Yet, despite these high expectations, a program must grasp the importance of the *process* of becoming a national champion rather than focusing simply on the trophy. On a daily basis, the team should be reminded of what they need to do in the practice gym to get them one step closer to playing in the championship game.

Situational Perception	Outcome Focus	Process Focus
Playing a lesser opponent	Beat the team badly because we are the better team	Outplay the opponent; take care of our side of the net by doing what we do
Playing a tough, close match	View tough matches as a threat—we may lose	View this as a challenge; we want to test our skills
Playing a highly ranked team	Going to be tough to beat this team	It's all about our side of the net—let's play our game
Playing a lesser opponent	Chances that our team will play down to their level due to over-confidence	Focus on playing our game and improve upon our weaknesses
Playing with a key starter injured	How can we compete? How can we win?	Now we really have to play together; what more can we each contribute?
Starting slow versus a lesser opponent	We can pick it up at any time	We have to get back to the game plan
Starting slow versus a tough opponent	What's going on? Finger-pointing, blaming, even panic	We have come back before; go back to the game plan
Playing with a new lineup	We need time to get used to each other: could be tough to get a win	Let's help each other play our team game
Playing a tough schedule	Going to be tough to go unde-feated; who can we beat?	Each game will challenge us to play to our utmost; we must be ready to play

Figure 14-3. What game do you play? Process versus outcome

These daily standards and goals are all part of the process of improving the team's ability to maximize their collective potential. Figure 14-3 illustrates the differences between an outcome focus and a process focus. Coaches who are always emphasizing the outcome focus are teaching their players that only a win can bring satisfaction and a sense of accomplishment. Teams that are coached with an outcome focus usually adopt the perceptions listed in Figure 14-3. For example, when they play against a weaker team, players can let their guard down and not play to their utmost abilities because they feel that that it will not be necessary. When these teams play against tough teams, some may perceive the match as a threat, since winning may not happen. With teams like these, there is no such thing as a "moral" victory—even if they play very well, they cannot give themselves credit because the outcome was not accomplished. Also, if adversity strikes, such as a starter getting hurt or playing with a new lineup, these players can get shaken because winning has been made even harder.

Conversely, process-orientated coaching can lead to more favorable perceptions by players. As mentioned several times throughout this book, winning is somewhat of an uncontrollable. A team that embraces the importance of the process puts the onus on themselves to play to their maximal capacities. Whether playing against lesser or better teams, process-orientated players take care of their own side of the net first, then let the outcome take care of itself. The focus is on improving the team's product (team performance), so if adversity strikes, such as injured starters, new lineups, or slow starts, the team is ready to continue their pursuit of playing well, one pass at a time. Teams like these do not feel threatened by higher-ranked programs; they actually look forward to the challenge of testing their play against the best. Helping players adopt this type of team philosophy takes time, continual follow-up, and productive feedback. Most players are coached under the win-at-all-cost professional sport model in their school and club teams, so they may be somewhat resistant to changing their mindset. But once players allow the "process" to guide them, they will begin giving themselves credit for good performances (regardless of outcome), and attempt to play better each practice and improve from one game to the next.

Figure 14-4. Winning championships takes a great understanding of the process of getting there, one practice at a time.

Rules without Relationships

Coaching today's athlete is much different than it was 20 years ago, or even 10 years ago. Anecdotal evidence includes feedback from coaches who consistently state that the one major difference between athletes from the past and today's athletes is the importance placed on the coach-athlete relationship (Voight, 2000c). "Rules without relationships lead to rebellion" is a popular title for presentations on the topic. Team rules and standards will not be accepted or adhered to if a real player-coach relationship is not developed. The relationship developed between the coach and his players must be based upon things beyond just athletic performance. This is not to say that the coach must now become a best friend to the players, but for players to give their all to the team and the coach, there must be something more to their bond than the volleyball court. Pete Carroll, head football coach at USC, stated that "the relationship is the best way to get the result. I'm convinced that developing and maintaining healthy relationships is the best way, if not the only way, to get where you want to go in life." Coaches at all levels of sport must put in the necessary time and effort to get to know their players as people and players. Coaches who invest in their players will have players who invest in the team pursuit and their coaches. Do not become one of the many coaches who learned this lesson the hard way—by having players quit on them, player revolt, team dissension, player dissatisfaction, and the team underperforming.

Teachable Moments: Productive Coaching

The term "teachable moment" was referred to in Chapter 13, yet it is important enough to repeat and expand upon here, especially in the youth sport setting. Finding moments when players do things right is a valuable teaching strategy, which is also referred to as productive coaching. When deserved, productive feedback can help positively influence a player's competence, self-confidence, and intrinsic motivation. Competence has been defined as a player's skill capabilities, as well as his knowledge of the intricacies of his sport. A player's self-confidence consists of his belief in his abilities. Most coaches believe that confidence is at the core of playing to potential. A player's intrinsic motivation refers to his drive for continued efforts at improvement and achievement. Coaches can have a profound influence on young competitors through productive coaching methods, specifically their instructional behaviors, use of keen observation, careful use of feedback, reinforcement, and motivation, and the development of a process-oriented team climate.

Instructional Behaviors

To be a more effective educator, follow the tips contained in this "teachable moment" checklist. An often-used coaching phrase is that "the game is the best teacher." Coaches should let players play rather than simply talk about how it should be done. Some coaches simply talk too much. To aid in educating players on the process, coaches can TARGET their practices:

T = Task: Use a variety of activities and exercises that are challenging, yet appropriate for the developmental and ability levels of the players.

A = Authority: Coaches should involve athletes in decision making, such as choosing some activities for practice and uniforms. Athletes at age 16 and older prefer coaches to train them in competitive drills and practices as well. They may want some say, but players at this age want the coach to dictate the standard and hold them to it.

R = Recognition: Coaches should reward individual improvement and effort, while at the same time focusing on the athlete's self-worth and confidence.

G = Grouping: Technical practice should move from individual, to small group, to large group work. The smaller the group, the more reps with the ball each player gets.

E = Evaluation: Individual standards of performance should measure progress, not simply outcome-based results such as winning or losing. Even in a loss, coaches should evaluate good aspects of play.

T = Timing: Coaches should provide time for learning and improvement by utilizing teaching progressions from simple to complex and providing "lots and lots" of reps. Time should be spent practicing, not standing in line waiting for a turn. Repetitions and overlearning is critical for younger players.

Courtesy of SCVC & Ralf's Photography

Figure 14-5. Competitive youth coaches can improve player execution by being *on target*.

Keen Observation

A coach should not only look for "teachable moments" and error correction opportunities, but instead be observing and listening for particular verbal and nonverbal statements and behaviors of players because they could be conveying important information—namely levels of competence, self-confidence, and persistence.

Coaches must be cognizant of statements made from players like "I can't do this," "I don't know what to do most of the time," or "I am so stupid." Players may be making these statements out of their frustration about not being competent enough to play on this team. Players must be told that learning their skills will take a lot of time and practice. Players must not be admonished for making mistakes at this level of play. Players should be able to use trial and continuous error correction without penalty (laps, getting yelled at). Getting on players backs will only have an adverse effect on their confidence and competence, and possibly drive them away from a game they once loved. In a similar vain, hearing talk like "I stink," or "I am the worst player on this court," could denote players who are really struggling with their confidence. Upon hearing this, you should attempt to get players to think about improving upon their last performance rather than comparing themselves with others, since they have no control over how their teammates or opponents play.

In terms of going too far with boosting player confidence, coaches should be cautioned about only praising worthy performances. You must be careful not to praise easy tasks that the player does in his sleep or it will leave him with the perception that you think he is not very skillful (i.e., that accomplishing an easy task is a challenge for him). Players at all competitive-age levels are very perceptive and are always looking for real or mixed messages from adults and coaches. A player's sense of competence and confidence is greatly enhanced when they accomplish challenging tasks. So coaches should continue to set high, yet realistic standards that their players could accomplish if they put forth their best effort.

Another issue for coaches to be aware of is when they notice that a player's effort is dropping off. When this occurs, it could be due to something going on at home or school, and this player is probably having trouble "letting go" or "moving on" from the issue. Having a rapport with your players will help them to open up when they do have problems. A decrease in work rate could also mean some dissatisfaction with you, your coaching, or their teammates. The sooner these issues can be discussed the better. The player could easily be getting some "bad" information or "misperceptions" from their parents, so both parties should be addressed so there is no further miscommunication. Players may begin to miss practices and games (with faulty excuses) as a way of avoiding a threatening situation, such as a problem with a teammate or you, the coach, or because of a fear of making mistakes or letting his parents down. Getting a player to talk about how things are going is very important.

Players who avoid playing could also be close to being on their way out. They may not be getting what they want from the experience, such as a relationship with coaches or teammates, improved play, or challenging play. Find out why your players play, so you can be in a better position to help them meet their expectations and preferences.

Feedback and Reinforcement

To improve upon the use of contingent praise, it is important to offer the type of praise that gives players a standard to achieve while providing skill-relevant feedback. General feedback, like "nice job," is not even close to providing important information. Feedback such as, "You passed the ball right where it needed to be for that particular play. Let's try that again," is much better and much more informative. The following list includes tips you can follow to improve upon the use of productive feedback.

- Use "I" messages instead of "you" messages. This helps to reduce a defensive stance from the player. For example, "I see you not getting into platform quick enough."
- Sarcasm has no place in a learning environment.
- Reward what you want, not what you do not want. Sometimes ignoring something negative will take care of it, especially if the player is not getting the attention he is looking for. If this is not possible, try and step in without making a big deal, devoting as little time as possible. Attention is what athletes want most of the time, so it is best if they see you giving your attention and positive feedback to those players doing the right things, and not devoting much time to those individuals doing the wrong things.
- Watch how you offer coaching points, like pointing your finger at players with a demanding tone, facial expression, or body language that emits a negative connotation. The *message* may be great but the player may not be listening because they are too distracted by the nonverbals ("Why is he so mad at me?"). What coaches do and how they do it speaks volumes, more so than what they actually say.

The best way to motivate players is to keep them working on improving their game every day, as well as by doing the following:

- Get to know your players and give them some time outside of volleyball (ask them about school, family, interests, etc.).
- Plan ways to improve team cohesion and increase motivation (it will not just happen).
- Have training sessions that are organized, competitive, and full of reps.
- Establish a standard for practice behaviors and hold players accountable to them. If the team standard is to not allow the ball to hit the floor without having a body flying after it, then that should be the consistent standard, day in and day out. Once coaches allow a ball to drop without a "punitive reminder," the standard has been

lowered. With each occasion of the ball dropping, the standard will be dropped even lower.

- Establish roles and responsibilities for each player. Once every player feels like a contributing member of the team, good things will happen.
- If the situation dictates, showing players your frustration and disappointment can be beneficial (will show them you care), yet coaches should never attack a player's personality or character.

The following list details how coaches should not attempt to motivate their players. By using these methods and feedback, coaches may see an immediate behavior change, based upon fear and resentment from the players, but this will reap havoc on the coach's character, credibility, and future leadership ability.

- Intimidation ("If you don't go out and play hard I will cut you.")
- Threats ("If you make the same mistake again you won't play for a long time.")
- Criticism and sarcasm ("That's the worst volleyball I have ever seen." "My five-year-old knows volleyball better than all of you combined.")
- Guilt ("All the time I've put in training you and this is what I get in return.")
- Physical abuse ("We'll run the entire next practice if...")
- Fear ("I want them to fear me because they work harder.")
- Arrogance ("I am the coach—what can one of my players tell me that I don't already know?")
- Negativity ("I'm doing my players a big favor by treating them like this—it is preparing them for the real world.")
- Favoritism ("Every good coach treats his better players differently from the rest.") It is important for coaches to tell their players that everyone will be treated fairly. It is very difficult to treat each player equally, so coaches should focus on developing a relationship and rapport with each team member and try and be as fair as possible with them.
- Chapter 10 addressed some of these points in the 10 Commandments of Team Communication.

Team Climate

It is important for coaches to develop their own coaching philosophy and vision for the team, which together should act as a compass for coaches as they embark on the journey of leading their team. Ask yourself such questions as "What is my coaching philosophy? What is the main *goal* of my coaching? What is the goal for the season?" It is hopeful that player development, fun, and skill improvement make up the top three coaching goals and priorities, especially for youth coaches. These goals should not only be passed onto the players and their parents, but they should also be practiced and enforced during every practice and game. Making sure that every player plays, is involved with each drill, is given opportunities for practice reps, and is given appropriate reinforcement (in proportion to the difficulty of the skill or activity) are ways of putting these standards to work. Other elements to an effective team climate include error correction (how coaches help players learn from mistakes), and post-game/post-practice evaluations.

"We're constantly trying to bring up the last one-third of our team to a higher level. We feel that the better the last third gets, the better practices we're going to have and the better our first team is going to get."
—Mick Haley, Head Women's Volleyball Coach, USC
(Anderson, 2003, p. 18)

How a team treats each other, especially the reserve players, can make a great difference in their effectiveness. As stated above, Mick Haley, who has won national titles at Texas and USC, stresses the importance of challenging every player, especially the reserves. Anson Dorrance, a highly successful women's soccer coach at UNC, also highlights the need for teams to respect their reserves, as they are the foundation of any competitive program. Coach Dorrance has said that the treatment of reserve players is one of the key components of team chemistry and effective leadership. Some important questions to ask of yourself and your team include:

- What are the attitudes of the reserve players?
- Are reserve players respected for their contributions?
- How do the starting players view and treat reserve players?
- How do you (as the coach) treat your reserve players compared to how you treat your starters?

The answers to these questions could be at the heart of your successes or failures.

Post-Game Evaluations

A valuable teachable moment that often goes by without notice or without being used effectively enough is the post game/post practice evaluation. Both players and coaches can best utilize this time to take note of:

- What they are feeling and thinking about their performance
- What got them to the outcome (good, neutral, or poor)
- How the play was compared with play in the past (improvement, neutral, or "back a few steps")
- What aspects of the "team" game were good, neutral, or poor
- What specific aspects will need to be targeted during training

How these points are addressed, attributed, and emphasized to players can have a profound effect (good or bad) on the athlete's interpretation of the outcome, which then strongly influences mindset, attitude, and motivation for future performance (practice and game play). For example, a loss can still be a desirable outcome if the team gave all they had and improved in certain areas of emphasis; the opposite applies to a "sloppy" win in which the team simply went through the motions and did not work hard or improve their team game, yet still got the outcome. Coaches set this tone with their post-game feedback. Sport psychologist Mark Anshel (1990) wrote, "Coaches are responsible for making an honest and accurate evaluation of good and poor performance so that the causes of the end result can be objectively determined." Some common examples of how coaches assess the causes of the outcome (win, loss) could include (Anshel, 1990):

- Ability Attributes
    "We played well today."
    "We've been jump-serving great recently."
    "We did not play well at this tournament."
    "We are mentally tougher than most teams."

- Task Difficulty Attributes
    "We really battled against their big block today, but it was just too big."
    "Their setting was just the best I have seen in a long time."
    "We played well despite playing against players two years older."
    "We just beat one of the best teams at this tournament."

- Effort Attributes
    "We were outworked this game."
    "When we go after every ball we are tough to beat."
    "We have to be aggressive to win this championship."
    "We didn't put the effort in during practice this week to adequately prepare."

- Luck Attributes
    "Luck was not on our side today."
    "The officials were making all the wrong calls today."
    "That team pulled off some 'career' shots today."
    "We just didn't have it today."

The research that has been conducted on success and failure attributions has revealed much about how students and athletes perceive what they are being told and how these perceptions relate to their future actions. For example, younger athletes who attribute losses/failure/undesirable outcomes to *low ability* tend to have higher levels of anxiety, lower levels of confidence, and are more at risk to drop out of sport. Also, athletes who continually attribute, or are told by their coaches, that losses are due to their lack of *ability* or *bad luck* tend to lose motivation and drive to continue striving to practice and perform. It is wiser to attribute undesirable outcomes (losses, poor performances with a win) to *low effort*, since players can always change this, or to *luck* and the opponents' *ability*.

Help players realize that unsuccessful performances can also be attributed to inadequate training, a lack of continual effort throughout the match, inappropriate strategy, or an inadequate focus in critical times—and that these are all *internal* attributes that can be changed. Coaches who continually attribute losses to low ability will de-motivate their players and lead to more inconsistent, poor play. Most athletes perform better in future contests when they attribute a negative outcome to effort rather than ability. Attributing failure to ability again leads to lower confidence and a decreased motivation to continue putting in effort. Effort should always be mentioned as the most important factor in skill improvement. If skill is emphasized too much, those athletes who are not as skilled as the others will assume that they "don't have it'" and never will.

Coaches must be careful about getting too involved in blaming outside forces for losses and failures, such as luck, officiating, or the superior opponent. Although it was stated earlier that attributing losses to outside factors can protect younger players' sense of competence and confidence, if outside factors are always mentioned as the cause of a loss this can de-motivate athletes in the long run. Players may feel good at the time to get past the loss, but if they keep hearing about this "impossible opponent" they will begin to question their ability. Again, external factors like luck and a tough opponent can be cited sparingly to save a team's ego and confidence, if that is deemed important, such as after a great match in which the team battled tremendous adversity to keep the game close. If coaches elect to use external factors like luck and task difficulty, they should try and state this in positive terms, such as: "We played OK today—the opponents just pulled out some lucky shots" (luck); or "Hold your heads high—you were beat by a very good team today" (task difficulty).

As mentioned by Figure 14-1, coaches should be aware of the developmental considerations of their players, especially with regards to comparing one player to another (social comparison). There are only a few athletes who actually can take being compared to other players ("Why can't you serve like Torie?). Most athletes will question their own ability instead of getting motivated to work harder to play like Torie. It should not be a problem to tell an athlete that they are not starting and Torie is starting due to some objective performance criteria, because this helps the athlete to understand the specific areas in which they are deficient. Subjective statements hurt players personally, and then adversely affect their confidence and motivation to continue to play.

Finally, coaches must be honest and real with their time-out/game-break/post-game comments. If players failed to execute the skills, let them know rather than blaming luck or citing a good opponent all the time. The important point here is that coaches need to think about what to say and what message they want to get across. When coaches let their emotions run the show, and say what will make them feel better (cathartic coaching), they may lose several players when all is said and done. As stated earlier, coaching today's athlete is very different from the Bob Knight days of yelling, pushing, and cajoling. Players want to be treated with respect and given responsibility. Especially during time-outs and post-game evaluations, coaches' attributions should be phrased in terms that educate, as in, "We need to do a better job of getting to every down ball," rather than in terms that attack and destroy, as in "You could not have beaten the U12's today."

Final Thoughts

A sport like volleyball demands a lot from its participants. Especially with the rally-scoring system, every technical miscue and mental mistake leads to a point, which could come back to haunt teams late in game five. This game can be a tremendous test for players because of the momentum swings and the importance of every serve, pass, and swing. Players and teams who are able to let go of the previous play and focus on the next serve will have an advantage over most of their opponents. Players and teams who are able to put in quality, consistent training sessions will be at an even greater advantage.

Figure 14-6. Volleyball can elevate players to great heights and experiences.

By helping your players become mentally tougher, you will enable them to become comfortable being uncomfortable, remain confident, composed, and resilient, and be able to train with consistent focus and effort. For some players these skills are automatic. But for the majority of players these skills must be practiced, much like passing, serving, and hitting. Once players are able to incorporate these mental skills on a daily basis without hesitation, they are well on their way to performing to their potential. Once this occurs, players will be able to achieve great things, like playing to the best of their ability, playing on teams that play for each other, winning a championship or two, and maybe even making a visit to the White House.

References and Recommended Reading

Anderson, R.J. (2003). Sweat & smiles. *Coaching Management*, 11(9), 18–22.

Anshel, M.H. (1990). *Sport Psychology: From Theory to Practice*. Scottsdale, Ariz.: Gorsuch Scarisbrick, Publishers.

Baechle, T.R. & Earle, R.W. (2000). (Eds.) *Essentials of Strength Training and Conditioning*. Colorado Springs, Colo.: NSCA.

Baechle, T.R., Earle, R.W., & Wathen, J. (2000). Resistance training. In T.R. Baechle & R.W. Earle (Eds.) *Essentials of Strength Training and Conditioning* (pp. 395–426). Colorado Springs, Colo.: NSCA.

Beal, D. (2004). Setter training. In K. Lenberg (Ed.) *Coaching Volleyball: Offensive Fundamentals and Techniques* (2nd edition, pp. 78–84). Monterey, Calif.: Coaches Choice Publishers.

Beal, D. (2002). Seeking excellence in a program—going for the gold. In D.Shondell & C. Reynaud (Eds.) *The Volleyball Coaching Bible* (pp. 37–52). Champaign, Ill.: Human Kinetics.

Bompa, T. (1983). *Periodization of Training*. Champaign, Ill. Human Kinetics.

Bowden, B., Bowden, T., & Brown, B. (1996). *Winning's Only Part of the Game*. New York, N.Y.: Warner Books.

Braden, J. (2002). Finding direction and inspiration amidst ups and downs. In D.Shondell & C. Reynaud (Eds.) *The Volleyball Coaching Bible* (pp. 28–41). Champaign, Ill.: Human Kinetics.

Carron, A.V., Spink, K.S., & Prapavessis, H. (1997). Team building and cohesiveness in the sport and exercise setting: Use of indirect interventions. *Journal of Applied Sport Psychology*, 9, 61–72.

Chichester, B. (2002, Spring). The dangers of dehydration. *Hydrate*, 11.

Didenger, R. (1995). *Game Plans for Success*. Chicago, Ill.: Contemporary Books.

Dorfman, H. (2003). *Coaching the Mental Game*. Lanham, Md.: Taylor Trade Publishing.

Dorrance, A. (1996). *Training Soccer Champions*. Raleigh, N.C.: JTC Sports.

Dufresne, C. (2004, May). Revolution stops here. *Los Angeles Times*, D 12.

Emma, T. (2003). *Peak Performance Training for Sports*. Monterey, CA: Coaches Choice Publishers.

Fishman, M.G., & Oxendine, J.B. (1998). Motor skill learning for effective coaching and performance. In J.M. Williams (Ed.) *Applied Sport Psychology: Personal Growth to Peak Performance* (3rd edition: pp. 13–27). New York, N.Y.: Macmillan.

Fitzgerald, M. (2003, August). The top 10 sports science tips. *Triathlete*, 56–59.

Hardy, C.J., & Crace, R.K. (1997). Foundations of team building: Introduction to team building primer. *Journal of Applied Sport Psychology*, 9, 1–10.

Henschen, K.P. (1986). Athletic staleness and burnout: Diagnosis, prevention, and treatment. In J.M. Williams (Ed.) *Applied Sport Psychology* (pp. 327–342). Palo Alto, Calif.: Mayfield.

Hydrate (2002, Spring). Power up with H_2O, 18.

Janssen, J. (2002). *Championship Team Building*. Cary, N.C.: Winning the Mental Game.

Jenkins, R. (2003). Mental preparation for quarterbacks. www.TopGunQBAcademy.com

Jordan, M. (1994). *I Can't Accept not Trying*. New York, N.Y.: HarperCollins.

Kluka, D. (2004). *Talent Identification*. Presentation book at AVCA national convention. Long Beach, Calif..

Lencione, P. (2002). *The 5 Dysfunctions of a Team*. New York, N.Y.: Macmillan.

Liddane, L. (2002, February 4). Feed your muscles. *Daily News*, 42.

Loehr, J. (1994). *The New Toughness Training Manual for Sports*. New York, N.Y.: Plume-Penguin.

Loehr, J., et al. (October, 2001). Workshop presented at the Association for the Advancement of Applied Sport Psychology, Orlando, FL.

Los Angeles Times. 2005, April 28. D1.

Los Angeles Times. 2004, November 27. D2.

Los Angeles Times. 2003a, September 24. D12.

Los Angeles Times. 2003b, July. D3.

Los Angeles Times. 2003c, August 30. D10.

Los Angeles Times. 2003d, October 31. D2.

McCallum, J. (2001). The gang's all here. *Sports Illustrated*, 75–81.

McCann, S. (2002). A model of offensive and defensive mental skills. *United States Olympic Coach*.

McKown, M., & Malone, K. (2003). *Strength Training with Dumbbells*. Germany: Myers and Myers.

Moore, B. (1998). Confidence. In M.A. Thompson, R.A. Vernacchia, & W.E. Moore (Eds.) *Case Studies in Sport Psychology* (pp. 63–88). Dubuque, Iowa: Kendall/Hunt Publishing.

Murphy, M. (1996). *The Achievement Zone: 8 Skills for Winning all the Time—From the Playing Field to the Boardroom*. New York, N.Y.: G.P. Putnam's Sons.

Nideffer, R. (1989). *Attentional Control Training for Sport*. Los Gatos, Calif.: Performance Services.

Nideffer, R. (1976). Test of attentional and interpersonal style. *Journal of Personality and Social Psychology*, 34, 394–404.

Potach, D.H. & Chu, D.A. (2000). Plyometric training. In T.R. Baechle & R.W. Earle (2000). (Eds.) *Essentials of Strength Training and Conditioning* (pp. 427–470). Colorado Springs, Colo.: NSCA.

Orlick, T. (2000). *In Pursuit of Excellence* (3rd ed.). Champaign, Ill.: Human Kinetics Publishers.

Osbourne, T. & Ravizza, K. (1988). Nebraska's 3 R's: 1 play-at-a-time pre-performance routine for collegiate football. *The Sport Psychologist*, 5, 256–265.

Reimers, K. & Ruud, J. (2000). Nutritional factors in health and performance. In T.R. Baechle & R.W. Earle, R.W. (Eds.) *Essentials of Strength Training and Conditioning*. Colorado Springs, Colo.: NSCA.

Riley, P. (1993). *The Winner Within*. New York, N.Y.: Putnam.

Roberts, P. (2001, May). Ed Burke's got a rocket in his pita pocket. *Outside*, 87.

Saindon, B. (2004). Linear and non-linear passing performance: A dialogue among coaches. In K. Lenberg (Ed.) *Coaching Volleyball: Offensive Fundamentals and Techniques* (2nd ed., pp. 221–226). Monterey, Calif.: Coaches Choice Publishers.

Schmidt, A., Peper, E., & Wilson, V. (2001). Strategies for training concentration. In J. Williams (Ed.) *Applied Sport Psychology* (4th ed.; pp. 333–346). Mountain View, Calif.: Mayfield.

Schmidt, R.A. & Wrisberg, C.A. (2000). *Motor Learning and Performance* (2nd ed.). Champaign, Ill.: Human Kinetics.

Shondell, D. & Reynaud, C. (Eds.) (2002). *The Volleyball Coaching Bible,* Champaign, Ill.: Human Kinetics.

Silva, J. (1990). An analysis of the training stress syndrome in competitive athletics. *Journal of Applied Sport Psychology,* 2, 5–20.

Smith, D. (1999, September). Overtraining in sport. Symposium presented at the annual meeting of the Association for the Advancement of Applied Sport Psychology Annual Conference, Banff, Canada.

Stellino, V. (2002, October). Jags try positive approach. *Florida Times Union,* D 10.

USA Today (2003, October 17). Viking players have become true believers in what their coach says, 2C.

USC Hospitality Services Pamphlet (2003).

Vealey, R. (2002). Sport confidence from a social-cognitive perspective: Extending and blending research and practice. Presented at October AAASP Conference, Tuscon, Ariz.

Voight, M.R. (2004). Offensive and defensive mental skill survey. *Coaching Volleyball,* 2, 15-18.

Voight, M.R. (2003). Combating training stress syndromes to improve the quality of strength and conditioning training and performance. *Strength and Conditioning Journal,* 11, 22–29.

Voight, M.R. (2002). Improving the quality of practice: Coach and player responsibilities. *Journal of Physical Education, Recreation, & Dance,* 73, 43–48.

Voight, M.R. (2001). A team building intervention program study with university teams. *Journal of Sport Behavior,* 24, 420–431.

Voight, M.R. (2000a). When the work doesn't get done: Important consequences for players and coaches. *Coaching Women's Basketball,* 1, 12–13.

Voight, M.R. (2000b). Postseason play: Mentally preparing for the distractions. *Coaching Women's Basketball,* 2, 10–12.

Voight, M.R. (2000c). *A structural model of the determinants, personal and situational influences, and the consequences of athlete dissatisfaction.* Unpublished dissertation. University of Southern California.

Waite, P. (2002). Giving players and teams the competitive edge. In D. Shondell & C. Reynaud (Eds.) *The Volleyball Coaching Bible* (pp. 300–325). Champaign, Ill.: Human Kinetics.

Walsh, B. & Dickey, G. (1990). *Building a Champion*. New York, N.Y.: St. Martin's Paperbacks.

Williams, P. (1997). *The Magic of Teamwork*. Nashville, Tenn.: Thomas Nelson Publishers.

Woods, T. (2001). *How I Play Golf*. New York, N.Y.: Macmillan Publishers.

Yukelson, D. (1997). Principles of effective team building interventions in sport: A direct services approach at Penn State University. *Journal of Applied Sport Psychology*, 9, 73–96.

Ziegler, S. (2002). Attentional training: Our best kept secret. *Journal of Physical Education, Recreation, and Dance*, 73, 26–30.

Additional Resources

National Strength and Conditioning Association
www.nsca-lift.org

International Center for Sports Nutrition
(402) 559-5505

Nutrition Counseling Education Services
www.ncescatalog.com

Association for the Advancement of Applied Sport Psychology
www.aaasponline.org

Sport Psychology Consulting
www.drmikevoight.com

About the Author

Mike Voight, Ph.D., CSCS, is a premier sport psychology-performance consultant with extensive experience working with athletes and teams from all types and levels of competitive sport. Mike has had the privilege of working with many collegiate, elite, Olympic, and professional athletes. Some notables include college and professional national champions, junior/national team soccer and volleyball players, Olympic athletes from diving, figure skating, and volleyball, and professional athletes from volleyball, hockey, basketball, soccer, and golf, as well as a Heisman trophy winner.

Mike is a senior lecturer in the Physical Education Department at the University of Southern California, and a part-time lecturer in the kinesiology department at California State University, Fullerton. He has also been the sport psychology-performance consultant for USC for seven years, having worked with athletes and coaches from volleyball, football, basketball, soccer, rowing, golf, tennis, swimming, water polo, and diving teams. Recently, one of his teams, the USC women's volleyball team, repeated as the 2002 National Champion. Being a certified sport psychology consultant (AAASP), a certified strength and conditioning specialist (CSCS), and a former Division I collegiate coach, Mike integrates the most recent research and applications from the sport sciences to provide the most comprehensive, cutting-edge performance enhancement programming.

Along with his private consulting practice in the greater Los Angeles area, Mike has been a speaker and consultant to top Division I universities throughout the nation, including Harvard, University of Texas, Vanderbilt, Oregon State, UNC-Charlotte, CAL, Rutgers, UMASS, and UT Chattanooga. Dr. Voight has been fortunate to consult with some of the best coaching staffs from the collegiate and professional ranks, most notably the coaching staffs from the New York Liberty and Washington Mystics (WNBA).

Dr. Voight also spends considerable time conducting sport performance–related research and presenting his applied work at national and international conferences. His published articles can be found in sport psychology, sport science, and coaching journals. He is an editorial board member for a sport science journal, and a reviewer for two applied research journals. Additionally, he is the series editor for a complete line of mental toughness training books through *Coaches Choice Publishing*. An educator, researcher, presenter, writer, and applied practitioner, he is listed in the United States Olympic Committee's Sport Psychology Registry.

Mike resides in Redondo Beach, California with his wife, Jenny, their son Bradley Cole, and their newborn twins, Allyson Eileen and Julieann Morgan.